D0679229

Religion in America

ADVISORY EDITOR

Edwin S. Gaustad

THE ASPECTS OF RELIGION
IN
THE UNITED STATES OF AMERICA

[Isabella Lucy Bird Bishop]

ARNO PRESS
A NEW YORK TIMES COMPANY
New York • 1972

Reprint Edition 1972 by Arno Press Inc.

RELIGION IN AMERICA - Series II
ISBN for complete set: 0-405-04050-4
See last pages of this volume for titles.

Manufactured in the United States of America

Library of Congress Cataloging in Publication Data

Bishop, Isabella Lucy (Bird) 1831-1904.
    The aspects of religion in the United States of
America.

    (Religion in America, series II)
    Reprint of the 1859 ed.
    1. U. S.--Religion. I. Title.
BR515.B57 1972   209'.73   75-38438
ISBN 0-405-04059-8

THE ASPECTS OF RELIGION IN

THE UNITED STATES

OF AMERICA.

THE

ASPECTS OF RELIGION

IN THE UNITED STATES

OF AMERICA.

BY THE AUTHOR OF

"THE ENGLISHWOMAN IN AMERICA."

LONDON:

SAMPSON LOW, SON, AND CO.

47, LUDGATE HILL,

1859.

CONTENTS.

THE ASPECTS OF RELIGION IN
THE UNITED STATES.

Chapter I.—*Introductory.*

HE " great revival " in America is now admitted as a fact by men of all parties. After making every due allowance for " exaggerations," and the warm colouring of " enthusiasm," it is recognized, as among the most noteworthy phenomena of the day, that the influence of the Holy Spirit has been felt during the past eighteen months in the United States to an extent unprecedented in any other country or period. To deny it would be blindly to reject the concurrent testimony of some of the most enlightened and sober-minded men in America. This revival still attracts deep interest among Christians of all denominations who desire the triumph of the gospel, and who recognize in the spread of Protestant Christianity the true germ of universal brotherhood; and it naturally leads to an inquiry into the state of the Transatlantic Churches, and of religion generally, in a country whose characteristics differ so widely from our own. These questions present themselves to many minds: What is the external influence of religion in the States? What is the attitude of the Churches with respect to slavery? What is the general style of preaching? What is the practical working of the national system of education? In what degree may a revival be regarded as the effect of any system which is pursued? Along with many others. There is also in England an admitted inability to reconcile the many discrepancies which America presents; as, for instance, a faithful ministry with the unrebuked sin of slavery; a prevalent religious influence with wide-spread political corruption; a correct standard of morality with the acquittal of Sickles by a Washington jury; Churches with highly orthodox standards of theology, and error and infidelity rampant; a complete system of education, and the grossest superstition and fanaticism; a revival more prolific in conversions than any modern age has witnessed with acts of lawlessness and wrong which would have been a disgrace to any community even in the dark ages themselves.

To all men of thinking minds there is much interest in an inquiry into the religious state of a mighty Protestant nation. It is a question of political as well as of religious importance; for on the influence which religion and that pure morality which is its offspring exercise upon a people who are unwilling to submit to any other restraints will depend the character of the part which America is destined to play in future history. Several large works of great research on the subject of religion in America have been written within the last few years abounding in valuable information; but they are too voluminous and too philosophical to come within the province of the general reader. In the limits of a work which will scarcely occupy two hours in the perusal, I propose to review the aspects of religion in America; namely, the condition of the Churches and their influence upon the world which is outside

their pale; examining the subject in that candid
spirit which its nature demands, neither depre-
ciating such advantages as the Churches may
possess over those of an older country, nor
palliating the defects which a careful inspection
compels us to recognize. It is a matter of re-
gret that so much prejudice still exists against
America. It is full time that old jealousies
should be buried, and that in a larger faith and
a more comprehensive charity the children
should forget the separation of their sires. The
data on which these chapters are founded were
obtained during a residence of more than a year
in the United States, from which I have only
recently returned; and I am much indebted to
Baird's valuable work on Religion in America
for correct statistical information.

CHAPTER II.—*Sectional Characteristics of the United States.*

N order to make the subject more interesting and intelligible to those who have not had the leisure to make themselves acquainted with the sectional characteristics of America, it is necessary to introduce it by a few explanatory remarks.

America cannot, in any sense, be viewed as a whole. She has the stimulating air of the Hudson's Bay regions and the enervating atmosphere of the tropics, each exerting its influence on the various races of her inhabitants. The vegetable productions of all latitudes, and the mineral wealth of all lands, are to be found within her limits. More tongues are spoken within her borders than Rome ever compelled to subjection. More races are congregated

under her flag than ever met under the same
equal government. From the period of her
discovery, downwards, she has been the goal of
many an exodus, religious and political, from
many lands, each one stamping its impress to a
greater or less extent. To her the eyes of the
" oppressed nationalities" of the old world have
perennially turned, recognizing her destiny as
the empire of the future; and when the liber-
ties of nations have been crushed not only by
overwhelming armies, but by the dead weight
of institutions, and customs, and prejudices,
which centuries had heaped upon them, and
which a moment of enthusiasm, however sublime, could not destroy, then instinctively have
the more aspiring spirits sought the shores of
the United States, exulting in the idea of freedom to carry out their own theories unbiassed
by the disastrous influence of traditional notions. The men who have left the deepest
mark upon America were men who had learned
the sense of their responsibilities to themselves
and to each other in the severe school of suffering, and who expatriated themselves to obtain man's inalienable right—freedom to worship God according to the dictates of his own

conscience. There were others who emigrated with the idea of forming feudal empires, some who sought to carry out proscribed political theories; the persevering Dutch, the volatile French, the sturdy English, and the rugged Scotch, leading the van of civilization in the New World. The perusal of the history of American colonization will amply repay the reader, and be a key to the comprehension of much that now appears inexplicable.

Partly in consequence of these early differences there is an absence of the homogeneity which exists in England; each part of which may be gauged by the same rule and standard, and where the religious type is to a great extent moulded by the existence and influence of a National Church. We must regard America as a gigantic confederation of sovereign States, each possessing its governor, constitution, and laws; each one, as far as its internal policy is concerned, being completely independent of the Federal Government at Washington. That these States were colonised or settled at different times, by men of different races, habits, and creeds, and that each section continues to bear the impress of the principles of its founders, renders anything like a general view of the state of religion in America very difficult indeed. A division of the States into their three great natural sections of north, south, and west, will assist the reader to arrive at a tolerably just appreciation of the subject. To these three the " march of Empire" renders it desirable to add a brief notice of the " Far West." On each of these circumstances have stamped characteristics and peculiarities which permanently tinge and modify the aspects of religion as it exists in any one of these divisions.

The North, generally speaking, comprises the six New England States, New York, New Jersey, and Pennsylvania, but it is to the dominant characteristics of the true North, New England, that I shall hereafter peculiarly allude. The impress of the pious men who landed on Plymouth Rock in 1620 can still be recognized. All these pioneers professed religion, and with few exceptions they did honour to their profession, and regarded the glory of God above temporal aggrandisement. The second and more important New England colony was founded, in 1628, in the noble Bay of Massachusetts, for the express purpose of providing an asylum

for persons suffering in the Old World for conscience sake, and of extending the kingdom of
Christ in the New. These men were members
of the Church of England; but the Puritans
were not far behind, having heard that near the
setting sun they might enjoy a tranquillity to
which they were strangers at home; and the
noblest colony England ever sent out, consisting
of nine hundred persons, and commanded by
John Winthrop, one of the purest men in the
country, landed in Massachusetts in 1630. The
exalted piety of these colonists is represented
by the language of the younger Winthrop: " I
shall call that my country where I may most
glorify God." Many of them sacrificed wealth
at home, and went from " a paradise of plenty
into a wilderness of wants." Neither had they
at that time separated from the Church of England. On their landing the claims of religion
took precedence of all others, and not in temples made with hands, but under the spreading
trees of the old primeval forest, they first found
that freedom to worship God which they have
transmitted unstained to their posterity. In
the fear of God, and taking his Word as their
guide, within five years from the foundation of

the colony, they drew up a constitution which was to serve as a sort of *Magna Charta*, embracing all the fundamental principles of just government, and guaranteeing to man his noblest rights; and in fourteen years from its foundation the government was placed upon the footing on which it now rests. Emigrants seeking liberty of conscience rapidly arrived from Europe; friendly treaties were made with the aborigines; God was emphatically honoured; trade increased, and prosperity smiled upon the settlements. Such was the origin of the " Bay Colony" of Massachusetts, a colony not only destined to exercise a controlling influence over the other New England settlements, but over the whole of the vast empire that was yet to arise from the shores of the Atlantic to those of the Pacific.

The colonies of Connecticut, Rhode Island, New Hampshire, and Maine, were settled partly by offshoots from the Plymouth and Bay settlements, beginning as early as 1623, and partly by fresh arrivals from England. Their founders were men very much of the same character, with the exception of the settlers in Rhode Island, some of whom disliked the rigid religious laws and practices of Massachusetts, and fled thither out of hatred to the stern morality of the other colonies. The other bands of emigrants were led by men who laid the foundation of their civil government by simply covenanting that "all of them would be ordered by the rules which the Scriptures held forth to them." Purity of religious doctrine, freedom of religious worship, and the service and glory of God were proclaimed as the great ends of these enterprises. Of all these bodies of colonists the Plymouth settlers alone were Congregationalists. The religion of these emigrants was preeminently the religion of the Bible. It was the foundation not only of their faith but of their civil laws. It was a religion remarkably favourable to a system of liberal education, and set a great value on high attainments. It was a religion of high purposes, and had the twin objects of the conversion of the heathen, and the founding of an empire in which the truth of God should rule. Their religion favoured liberty of conscience as it was then understood, however imperfectly as compared with subsequent developments.

Such, in brief, is the history of the coloniza-

tion of New England, and the impress of these
noble-hearted Puritans can still be recognized
everywhere, transmitted through six generations. There is the same vigorous independence, the same indomitable love of freedom,
the same spirit of resistance to wrong, the same
continual appeal to the laws of morality and
right as laid down in Holy Scripture. The
indolence and the vices which are produced by
an enervating southern climate are unknown.
The most persevering industry can do little
more than wring a subsistence from the reluct-
ant rugged soil, therefore work is the condition
of existence, and none are degraded by labour.
The laws of New England are framed on the
old Puritan model, and are very strict; and
though the letter of the statute by which a
woman could be fined for " wearing a silk
gown contrary to Christian propriety " has been
long obsolete, its spirit lingered till within the
last few years among the mountains of Vermont·
and Maine.   In the country districts a marked
reverence for family ties and parental authority
is discernible, and throughout these States there
is an hereditary respect for the Sabbath, and a
strict observance of it, perhaps only equalled in

Scotland. The character of the early settlers has been thus remarkably preserved, partly in consequence of the paucity of inducements for immigration, except in the seaport cities; and New England in many districts presents the spectacle, seldom witnessed in a land of progression and change, of families cultivating the soil which has been possessed for generations by their ancestors.

Congregationalism became the " established " form of Church government about 1640 in New England, and though in the cities Episcopalian and other congregations are to be found, it is still all-powerful, and to its form of government and doctrine the masses of the people are very strongly attached. On entering more minutely upon the state of religion in New England we shall find some things which are unsatisfactory; but, partly owing to the somewhat isolated position of these States, arising from soil and climate, yet mainly to the influence of a pure faith and the upright though occasionally intolerant character of the early settlers, it is probable, that, as far as its morals are concerned, New England is the fairest portion of the world.

The second, and as it may be termed the

antagonistic section of America, is separated by
the strong demarcation line of slavery from both
the North and West. Its characteristics are
opposite to those of the first, and no rule by
which the religious state of either could be
judged would apply to it. Important portions
of the South still bear the unmistakable impress in manners and habits of thought of the
courtiers and gentlemen, many of them of dissolute lives, who were the early colonists, while
the French character is distinctly exhibited in
those states of the extreme South which were
colonised from France. While New England
was the chosen asylum of the Puritan " roundhead," and may be regarded as settled by the
Anglo-Saxon race, with its love of liberty, its
equal civil institutions, and its unpretending
manners, the South was colonised by men of
Norman extraction, with an aristocratic love of
feudal institutions, and priding themselves upon
dignity and elegance of demeanour. The South
became the retreat of the " cavalier" whose religion was the easy one of fashionable life,
while that of the " roundhead" proscribed even
innocent amusements, and opposed an uncompromising resistance to the " lust of the flesh,

and the lust of the eyes, and the pride of
life."

Virginia was the earliest in date of all the
Colonies. A year before the " Pilgrim Fathers"
sailed from England, its legislature, chosen by
the people, established the Episcopal Church.
The religious element entered in some degree
into the formation of the Colony, but it was an
intolerant element. Attendance at parish worship was required under severe penalties, and
the sacramental services were legally obligatory.
Quakers, Dissenters, and Romanists were prohibited from settling in the province, and all
people entering the Colony without having
been Christians in the countries they came
from were condemned to slavery ! The legislators were strenuous religionists, after the type
of Claverhouse and Laud. Later emigration
to Virginia was of a very doubtful character,
and consisted partly of dissolute courtiers and
gentlemen with lost reputations and desperate
fortunes, who left the impress of their manners
upon the land to which they expatriated themselves.

Maryland was planted by Lord Baltimore, as
a refuge for persecuted Romanists, on the

broad basis of toleration for all Christian sects,
and possessed the first government of modern
times which granted complete liberty to all
classes of Christians. The political power of
the State has, however, long since passed away
from the Roman Catholics. North Carolina
was colonised by emigrants from Virginia, some
of whom were driven out by the intolerance of
its laws. Puritans from England and emigrants from Barbadoes followed, but it was
more than half a century before religion received any attention. South Carolina was
colonised by a motley horde at first, but later
became a favourite retreat of the dissatisfied or
impoverished aristocracy of England. Many
dissenters also went out from England, carrying
with them intelligence and sobriety. The com-
panies who obtained both the Carolinas from
Charles II. professed to be actuated by " a lau-
dable and pious zeal for the propagation of the
Gospel;" but true religion owed little or nothing to them, and the manners of the court of
the Restoration were preserved by the *élite* of
both these States and Virginia. The colony
of Georgia was founded last of all by Ogle-
thorpe, a gentleman of the Cavalier school,

warmly attached to his King and his Church. He led over a mixed multitude to the low shores of the Savannah; poor debtors from English prisons, godly Moravians from Herrnhut, Highlanders from Scotland, and a few French from the sunny slopes of Dauphiny. Improvidence, the greed of gain, persecution, dissatisfaction, recklessness, and ambition, peopled the pioneer States of the South. The descendants of these early colonists gradually spread themselves westward, and a large French emigration occupied a portion of the shores of the Mexican Gulf.

Stability in institutions, in habits of thought, and in religious belief, is one of the most marked features of the South, and the various *isms* so rampant elsewhere have failed in effecting an entrance. The laws and constitutions of the South differ widely, both in principle and practice, from those of the Northern States, and are formed with especial reference to that all-powerful institution which, by holding in captivity 4,000,000 of an alien race, colours the whole complexion of customs, manners, and morals, and exercises a most important influence on the state of religion. There

C

is a homogeneity in the South, and a oneness of feeling not to be found elsewhere in America; but, as may be expected from the circumstances of its colonization, the influence of religion, the strictness of law, and the purity of morals which characterize New England, are, comparatively speaking, not discernible. There are orthodox standards of doctrine, with an admitted inconsistency of practice, the chivalry and the brutality of the middle ages, refinement of manners and laxity of morals, feudal institutions and democratic government, law weak and public opinion despotic.

The intermediate States, which I class with New England, deserve a passing notice. The " Empire State " of New York was settled by the Dutch, and afterwards offered an asylum to the persecuted Protestants of Britain, France, Germany, and Italy. The extraordinary rush of Irish, English, and German emigrants, has obliterated the Dutch characteristics, and New York does not possess any distinctive " nationality." New Jersey was settled by the Dutch and by colonists from New England, and shortly afterwards received a considerable number of Scotch and Irish emigrants, all of them Protestants. It is impressed by the distinctive New England element, and its people, in the main, are intelligent and virtuous. The important State of Pennsylvania was settled by William Penn in 1682; and, though his party was composed of Quakers, the principle of unlimited toleration on which the Colony was established soon made it the resort of people of all creeds and of none. Though the Quaker population now forms but a small minority in the State, the quiet Quaker influence is everywhere apparent. Harmony and tranquillity have marked the affairs of the province. No act of persecution or intolerance has ever disgraced its statute-book. Virtue and morality, the characteristics of its founders, still hold a marked sway over its mingled population. It is one of the most prosperous and quietly-progressive States in the Union, and it is hardly a matter of doubt that this prosperity is owing in great measure to the religion of the Bible in which its foundations were laid. The West, comprising Wisconsin, Illinois, Michigan, Ohio, Indiana east of the Mississippi, and the older. parts of Iowa and Minnesota, has features peculiarly its own. It has been settled partly by

God-fearing families from New England, who
constitute its leaven, partly by the overflow of
the adventurous youth of the Northern States,
partly by illiterate emigrants from Britain,
partly by deep-thinking and industrious hosts
from Germany, and partly by the renegade
outpourings of all Europe and all America, who
seek to find in a new country that freedom
from the restraints of religion and morality
which they could never secure in more settled
communities.   Happily the influence of the descendants of the Puritans leavens this heterogeneous mass, and to a certain extent the externals of religion and order prevail.

In the West the true genius of America is
discernible.   All nations are placed in the cru-
cible of her institutions and come forth Americans.   In the West, with unlimited space for
expansion, meet the vigorous elements of all
nations; the Anglo-Saxon, the leader in the
practical movement, with his spirit of enter-
prise, of daring independence and indomitable
perseverance ; the German, the original leader
in the movement of ideas, with his spirit of inquiry, and his quiet application ; the Celt, with
the impulsive vivacity of his race ; the Scandi-

navian, the Hollander, the Spaniard, the Italian,
all congregating where the back-woodman's
hatchet is the battle-axe of civilization, led
together by the irresistible attraction of free
principles to commence a new era in the history
of the world—to *create*—without destroying the
result of the progress of past periods. All the
social and national elements of the world are
represented in the West. Every people, every
creed, every class of society has contributed its
share to that mixture out of which is to grow
the great nation of the New World. It is true
that the Anglo-Saxon race maintains its ascendancy, but it is by *fusing* rather than *absorb-
ing* the other national elements. They modify
each other; but when we trace the amalga-
mating power to its source, we find it in PRO-
TESTANT CHRISTIANITY.

Yet further west of the Mississippi is the
"Far West," the border-land of civilization.
Here are gathered all nations, creeds, and
tongues into an heterogeneous confederacy.
The elements of stability are nowhere discerni-
ble. Every creed has its adherents, and every
Church its ministers, from Mormonism up-
wards. Every new idea which is let fall takes

root instantly in a congenial soil; and so great
is the chaos of creeds and the confusion of *isms*
that it seems hardly possible for any but the
Great Teacher to answer the question which
there, as elsewhere, man's heart is continually
propounding, " What is Truth?"   In the Far
West there is a continual progression—an increasing movement onwards.   Old systems are
discarded before new ones have been thought
out to fill the void.   Law is powerless, and
those restraints which are the safeguards of
society are to some extent unknown.   It is
ever in a state of seething commotion, its aspect
is that of a troubled sea without a shore.   Society is there resolved into its original elements.
Before these distant territories are organized,
and law and order can assert their supremacy,
the influence of religion is all that can be relied
upon to restrain the turbulence of that vast
wave of population which is moving westward
with ever accelerated speed, and whose surges
are even now breaking far, far away beyond
the Western Prairies, upon the Rocky Mountains, and the shores of the Pacific.

Thus the sectional characteristics of America
are the result, in the Northern States, of the

stern virtue that sought freedom, and nothing
but freedom, in which the original Puritan democracy planted its stern banner upon Plymouth Rock; in the Southern, of a motley
immigration of lordly merchants and men of
aristocratic ambition; in the Western, of the
restless and enterprising elements of European
and American society, meeting in unlimited
space, amidst institutions free as the air of
heaven.

CHAPTER III.— *The Churches of the*
United States.*

HE brief glance, in the preceding
Chapter, at some of the leading
characteristics of the three great
sections of America, shows that
circumstances exist by which the character of
the religious influence in each must be in a
great degree modified. These sectional differences are very little understood in England,
and America is judged of as a whole by the
apparent condition of any one of its component
parts. Thus those who are disposed to look
favourably on the state of the Republic will
judge of the religious condition of its boundless

---

* As this Chapter is mainly devoted to a statistical
account of the various Churches, and is especially intended for reference, it may be passed over by the
general reader.

territories by Sabbath-keeping, order-loving Massachusetts; while those who take the dark side will judge it from the ruffianism of a New Orleans or Washington mob, or from the unsettled state of Kansas, yet fresh from its baptism of blood and flame. There is less difference between Edinburgh and Boston than between Boston and Superior City or New Orleans. The dark-haired, hut-inhabiting Celts of the West of Scotland, and the stirring artizans of Manchester and Birmingham, have more in common than the descendants of the Puritans in the New England States and the reckless inhabitants of the new districts south-west of the Mississippi, and have more community of sympathy than either of these possess with the aristocratic feudal proprietors of Virginia and the Carolinas.

But even when these sectional differences are in some degree appreciated, the subject of religion in America is not entirely cleared from misapprehension. With respect to America and England, we are accustomed to compare rather than to contrast, and to suppose that society will be subjected to those religious influences which, as they exist with us, are only produced by a national Church. In America there is no national form of religion, or state-endowed Church, by which the vast community may be religiously bound together, and upon whose resources the whole population is at liberty to draw. The State recognizes all creeds, but patronises none. All denominations are on the same footing, and flourish or decay as they obtain the suffrages of the people. Complete religious toleration exists; every man is at liberty to worship God after his own fashion, or not to worship at all. Every man is protected in the quiet exercise of his religion. Truth stands on its own immutable vantage-ground, and the civil power is unable to interfere with rights of conscience and religious worship. From the absence of an Established Church many people infer the absence of faith. English people find it so hard to realize a *national* apart from a *governmental* religion. In transacting the affairs of government the Sabbath is recognized and respect for it enjoined. Congress adjourns over the Sabbath, and the *custom-houses* and all other public offices are shut during the whole day. Both Houses of Congress are regularly opened with prayer.

The government, from the time of its establishment, has repeatedly called upon the nation to observe days of fasting and prayer in times of national distress, and of thanksgiving for general mercies. Again, the government has authorized the employment of chaplains in the army and navy, and at this moment there are such in all large vessels of war. A Christian spirit is likewise shown in judicial affairs. Oaths are administered on the Bible; a belief in a future state of rewards and punishments is required, and the oath of an Atheist is rejected. It also appears in the readiness shown by Congress to make large grants of public lands for the support of seminaries of learning, asylums and hospitals, although aware that the institutions thus endowed were under the direction of decided Christians, who would give a prominent place in them to their religious views. Thus, though the promotion of religion does not directly belong to the general government, but to the States, it is neither hostile nor indifferent to the religious interests of the country. Without State assistance religion stands on its own foundation, and, as I hope to show, effectually wins the respect or love of all men by its own intrinsic merits. The constitutions of the several States are distinctively and emphatically Christian, and are founded, with few exceptions, on the great principles of the Bible.

Complete toleration is granted. As may be expected, error and fanaticism do not conceal themselves; the sects are numerous and subdivided; but it is a gratifying fact that the orthodox Churches everywhere have largely the ascendancy in point of numbers.* The voluntary system is fully carried out, and I am under the impression that all denominations are equally attached to it. As no funds are set apart by the State for the maintenance of religious worship, the clergy depend for their salaries upon their congregations, and in some instances these salaries are supplemented by private endowments, and in the West by subscriptions and " donation meetings." Possibly, with economy,

* Among the one hundred different denominations enumerated in the Census table, the following singular names occur, " Democratic Gospel, Ebenezer Socialists, New Lights, Tunkers, Superalists, Cosmopolites, Free Inquirers, Children of Peace, Inspired Church, Pathonites, Believers in God, Perfectionists, Spiritualists," and others equally remarkable.

all the ministers may live upon their salaries, but it is impossible that any can grow rich upon them. The American Churches have no inducements to offer in the shape of richly-endowed benefices or high temporal position; and there is no denomination which has the power to confer upon its ministers that *status* in society which belongs by immemorial usage to the clergy of the Church of England. Hence it may fairly be presumed that a desire to preach the Gospel is the great motive which impels men into the ministry in the orthodox Churches in the United States. Hence, also, the clergy, as a general rule, are taken from a different class in society from that which furnishes the clergy of the Church of England, and, with all the high attainments and education which many of them possess, not many of " *The Upper Ten Thousand* " are to be found within their ranks. It may surprise some people to read that a sum exceeding *five millions sterling* is annually raised in America for the support of religion!

In presenting a statement of the condition of the various denominations, I must mention that my only reliable *data* are those of 1855, since which period the increase in the number of communicants *has far exceeded in proportion the increase in population,* and the membership of the Churches is a very just criterion of the religious progress of the country. The recent " Awakening" has also materially affected the Churches. Owing to the felt necessity of imposing the restraints of religion upon the unsettled population of the Far West, and the praiseworthy efforts of the Tract, Home Missionary, and other Societies, assisted by the aggressive spirit of the Churches themselves, the Church, the Sabbath-school, and the Minister ever accompany the vast wave of population as it rolls westward; so that one-seventh may safely be added to the number of church edifices given in the census returns of 1850, viz. 38,183, or one for each 646 of the population. The American Churches may be divided into two great doctrinal divisions, the Calvinistic, embracing the regular Presbyterians, Evangelical Baptists, Episcopalians, Congregationalists, German Reformed, Dutch Reformed, Covenanters, Associate and Associate Reformed Churches, and the Arminian, comprehending the Methodists of all branches, Lutherans, Cumberland Presbyterians, and Moravians.

With reference to their forms of Church government, they range themselves in three great
divisions:—1. The *Episcopal*, comprising the
Protestant Episcopal Church, the Moravians,
and the Methodist Episcopal. 2. The *Presbyterian*, including the Presbyterians usually so
called, the Associate, and Associate Reformed,
the Dutch Reformed, the German Reformed,
the Covenanters, the Lutherans, and the Cumberland Presbyterians. 3. The *Independent*,
comprising the Congregationalists and the Evangelical Baptists. Not only may the numerous
Evangelical denominations be comprehended in
two doctrinal and three governmental divisions,
but under *one*, as far as regards their firm and
complete unanimity on the doctrine of the supremacy of Christ in his Church, and the un-
lawfulness of any interference with its doctrine,
discipline, and government on the part of the
civil magistrate. There is not a single Evangelical Church in America which does not vie
with the Free Church of Scotland in asserting
and maintaining the doctrine of the Headship
of Christ in his Church, and that from him only
comes all lawful rule and authority in the same.

The Episcopal Church, as it was the first in

point of time, deserves the first notice. It was originally an offshoot of the Church of England, and agrees with it in doctrine. Its formularies have been slightly altered since the Revolution, some objectionable phrases have been removed, and some very sensible abbreviations have been made. There are, as in England, three ranks or orders in the ministry. The Churches choose their own pastors, but their installation requires the consent of the bishop of the diocese. The churchwardens are chosen by the communicants. The Episcopal Church has divided the States into dioceses. The affairs of each diocese are regulated by an annual convention composed of the diocesan clergy and one or more lay delegates from each parish, elected by the people or appointed by the wardens and vestry, the clergy and laity forming one body, but dividing into two houses and voting separately whenever this is demanded. The Convention is under the presidency of the bishop, and a concurrent vote of both houses (when voting separately) is necessary before any measure can pass. A general Convention, by the Canons of which the Episcopal Church is governed, is held every three years. It is composed of clerical and lay

delegates from each diocesan Convention, who
form the house of delegates, and of the bishops
who form the house of bishops. Both houses
must concur before a proposed measure can
become law.

The Episcopal Church has thirty-eight Bishops, 1,714 clergy, and 105,350 communicants,
and three theological seminaries. Its growth
and prosperity are very marked. It has vitality
and energy in its whole extent, and a large
amount of piety both in its ministers and members. A large number of the most respectable
people in the country, especially in the cities
and in the South, are connected with it. The
conditions of its membership are certainly less
strict than those of the other bodies, and it
comprises within its pale much of the wealth,
position, refinement, and fashion of America.
Indeed, if I may be allowed the word, it has a
majority of the *æsthetical* part of the population.
Its flourishing condition rebuts the assertion
that Episcopacy cannot stand unconnected
with the State.

The Congregationalists predominate in New
England, where they are more numerous than
all the other sects united. They have no

standards of faith and order other than the Holy Scriptures. They recognize no Church as an organized body politic, except a body of believers statedly assembling for religious worship and communion. Congregationalism recognizes neither a Universal Church, as does Rome, or a National Church, as do England and Scotland; but each *congregation* of believers is a Church sovereign and independent of itself. Each Church exists by the consent of its members to walk together in obedience to the Gospel of Christ. Their discipline and conditions of membership are exceedingly strict. They disavow the name "Independent" and practise the communion of Churches. They have seven General Associations or General Conventions, which bodies meet annually and maintain the "bond of fellowship" by sending delegates to each other; but these associations have not the power of government. Under their ecclesiastical system, into the details of which I have not space to enter, they have enjoyed for 225 years a great purity of doctrine, fidelity of discipline, and continual prosperity. No Churches have done more for the advancement of religion, education, and morality, or have been more distinguished by that liberal and noble spirit which values throughout the world the common Christianity of all who hold " one Lord, one faith, one baptism." They have 2,327 ministers, 210,000 members, eight colleges, and six theological seminaries or departments.

The Regular Baptists, next to the two former, are the oldest of the branches of the Christian Church in the United States. They hold that immersion is the only scriptural mode of baptism. Each of their Churches possesses the right of licensing men to preach the Gospel and of ordaining elders, and is wholly independent as regards its interior government. Delegates from Baptist Churches meet for the purpose of mutual counsel and encouragement, but not for government. The Baptists adopt the Bible in theory as their only confession of faith, but in practice they have creeds which, although varying somewhat in expression, agree in the main, and are decidedly Calvinistic. Prior to the Revolution they were violently persecuted, and the era of the Independence of the Colonies is also that of their freedom from molestation. They are a most numerous and important sect, especially in the Southern States. They have

6,175 ordained ministers, 808,754 members, and ten theological seminaries. About one-fifth of the entire population of the United States is supposed to be connected with them.

The Presbyterian Church has a complete organization. Each congregation has its pastor, ruling elders, and deacons. The pastor is chosen by the people, but their choice is subject to several important limitations. When a meeting of those persons in a Church who contribute to the support of a minister, presided over by a pastor invited for the purpose, has been held, and the majority has agreed upon a candidate, a " call" is made out. This call is taken to the presbytery under whose care the congregation is placed, and it decides whether it shall be presented to the person to whom it is addressed. If they think that there is sufficient reason for withholding it, it is returned to the people, who must then proceed to a new election. If there be no objection, and the presbytery is satisfied of the piety and ministerial qualifications of the candidate, he is ordained, after a rigid examination of his motives and doctrines, in the most solemn manner with prayer and the laying on of hands. The elders are the representatives of the people, and are chosen by them for the discipline of the Church and other important offices. The deacons take charge of the poor. Each Church has thus an independent organization; but it is a part of an extended whole, living under a uniform ecclesiastical constitution, and subject to the control of the presbytery. The Presbytery consists of all the pastors and one elder from each session within certain defined limits. Its most important duty is the examination and ordination of candidates for the ministry, and its examinations are most strict. The Synod is but a larger presbytery and intervenes between the presbytery and General Assembly. The General Assembly is the highest judicatory of the Presbyterian Church, and the bond of union between its several parts. It is composed of an equal number of ministers and elders from each presbytery. Its power is great. It decides all appeals, reviews the records of the synods, gives its advice and instruction in all cases submitted to it, decides all controversies regarding doctrine and discipline, testifies against error, superintends the whole Church, represses schismatical contentions, and seeks to promote love and truth through the whole Presbyterian

body. No Church possesses a more complete
organization. It holds the Westminster Confession in its strictest sense. It has always
secured learning and orthodoxy in its ministry.
In its history, embracing a period of a century
and a half, no man who has rejected the Calvinistic system of doctrine has been allowed to
remain a minister of the Church; and not an
Arminian or Pelagian has ever been a recognized pastor of their body. They constitute
one of the most powerful religious influences
brought to bear upon the country, not only
from their Christian zeal and consistency, but
from the number of eminent theologians connected with their body, and the wealth, enlightenment, and philanthropy contained within
their pale. They have 3,828 ministers, 374,433
members, and ten theological seminaries.

The Methodist Episcopal Church is the
largest religious body in the United States, and
exercises a most potent influence over the community. It holds the doctrinal opinions of the
Wesleyan Methodists of England, and in all
important points its ecclesiastical economy is
identical with theirs. It was organized in
1784. It differs from the Methodist Church

in England in recognizing chief pastors under
the name of bishops. A bishop is elected by
the General Conference, to which body he is
amenable for his moral and official conduct. He
travels through the country superintending the
spiritual and temporal affairs of the Church,
presides in the Annual and General Conferences,
ordains such as are elected by an annual conference to the office of deacons and elders, and
appoints the preachers to their stations. Each
of these bishops has his own field, and they
meet at the General Conference. It must be
understood, however, that Methodist Episcopacy is an *office*, not an order. The organization
of this Church is very complete, and is especially calculated to bear upon the great masses
of the people. The land is covered with a net-
work of stations and circuits, and the Gospel is
carried into the most remote and thinly-peopled
neighbourhoods. They have 14,000 Churches;
but the number of their congregations meeting
in various places may probably be estimated at
nearly 40,000. Their itinerating ministers are
to be met with everywhere. No class or colour,
however despised, is outside the pale of their
ministrations. Like their great Master, they go

to " seek the lost." Although in some sections
of the country overhaste and extravagance may
occasionally tinge their proceedings, they are
characterized by fervid zeal, devotion, and perseverance; and to their organization, and to
the efficiency of their ministry, much of the religious prosperity of the States is undoubtedly
owing. They have 8,740 ministers, 1,593,794
members, and five millions and a half of the
population are supposed to be under their influence.

In 1844 this huge body divided on the question of slavery; but some of the Southern
Churches joined the Northern body. The
" Methodist Church North" has seven bishops,
235 presiding elders, 4,814 effective ministers,
783,353 members, and 823 home missionaries.
The " Methodist Church South" has six bishops,
131 presiding elders, 1,942 effective ministers,
271 home missionaries, and 596,852 members,
quite a number of whom are slaves. Eleven
colleges and twenty-one academic institutions
are connected with these two bodies. I have
attended their churches in almost every part
of the United States, and some of the most
powerful sermons that I have ever heard have
been from their pulpits.

The smaller orthodox bodies remain to be considered.

Smaller Episcopal.

MORAVIAN.—This Church has twenty-eight ministers, 3,500 members, and a population of about 12,000 souls under its instruction.

Smaller Baptists.

SEVENTH DAY BAPTISTS.—This is a worthy Sect, differing from the regular Baptists by maintaining that the seventh day is still the day to be observed as the Sabbath. They have seventy-seven ordained ministers, seventeen licentiates, 6,500 members, and about 40,000 persons under their influence.

FREE WILL BAPTISTS.—This Sect holds a general atonement, and dispenses with election and the other Calvinistic points. As their name imports, they are distinctively Arminian. They have 1,107 ordained ministers, 250 licentiates, and about 60,000 members.

DISCIPLES OF CHRIST, REFORMERS, OR CAMPBELLITES.—This Sect was founded by Dr. Campbell, a Scotchman, who left the Presbyterian Church in 1812. They dispense with creeds and confessions, formularies and books of discipline, and propose, by "avoiding the technical and artificial language of scholastic theology," to restore " a pure speech to the household of faith." This church is supposed to embrace about 320,000 persons.

ANTI-MISSION BAPTISTS.—They have 825 ministers, and 58,000 members.

GENERAL BAPTISTS.—This Sect has 15 ministers, and 2,189 members.

CHURCH OF GOD, OR WINEBRENNARIANS. —231 ministers, and 13,500 members.

TUNKERS.—200 ministers, and 8,000 members.

MENNONITES.—250 ministers, 36,000 members.

These two bodies are of German origin.

The Baptist Sects taken together have 9,476 ministers, and 1,318,469 members.

Smaller Presbyterian Churches.

CUMBERLAND PRESBYTERIANS. — This Church was constituted in 1810. It holds a middle ground between Calvinism and Arminianism, and differs from the other Presbyterian Churches in having adopted the *itinerating* system of the Methodists. It is a very flourishing body, and has 300 ministers, 480 licentiates, 100,000 members, and four theological seminaries.

REFORMED DUTCH CHURCH.—This Church dates from the colonization of New York by the Dutch; but the Dutch language has been completely abandoned by its ministers. Its standards are those of the Reformed Church of Holland, and are purely Calvinistic. It has always been remarkable for the ability and efficiency of its ministry. It is a highly respectable as well as a very wealthy body. It has 380 ministers, fifty licentiates, 36,297 members, and the number of individuals under its instruction is about 150,000.

ASSOCIATE CHURCH.—This Church was organized, and has been very much recruited, from Scotland. It has 164 ministers, fifty-six licentiates, 21,588 communicants, and one theological seminary.

ASSOCIATE REFORMED CHURCH. — This Church has 315 ministers, ninety licentiates, 40,000 members, and three theological seminaries.

REFORMED PRESBYTERIANS, OR COVENANTERS.—These are the descendants of the

persecuted Scotch Presbyterians who refused to
accede to the settlement of religion in 1688.
They rigidly adhere to the Westminster Confession and Longer and Shorter Catechisms,
and maintain that the " solemn league and cove-
nant " is binding upon them in all lands. They
are an isolated body, and refuse allegiance to
the constitution on religious grounds. This
refusal in time occasioned a controversy which
divided the body. They have fifty-nine ministers, eighteen licentiates, 7,000 members, and
one theological seminary.

GERMAN REFORMED CHURCH. — This
Church, which is an offshoot of one bearing the
same name in Germany, has a very important
field among the immense German population of
the Atlantic and Western States. It has recently made very rapid progress. It has 1,000
ministers, 110,000 members, and one theological
seminary.

THE LUTHERAN CHURCH is also a very important body. It has 1,000 ministers, 225,000
members, and eight theological schools. It differs from the Lutheran Churches of Europe in
entirely rejecting the authority of the fathers in
ecclesiastical controversy, in renouncing the

doctrine of consubstantiation, and in rejecting the remnant of private confession.

The whole group of Presbyterian Churches has 6,145 ministers, 8,116 churches, 696,318 members, thirty colleges, and twenty theological schools.

Smaller Methodist Churches.

A secession from the Methodist Church, under the leadership of a man of colour, occurred in 1816, and received the name of " The African Methodist Episcopal Zion Church." It has two bishops, 155 preachers, and 6,203 members.

Another secession took place, in 1819, under the name of " The African Methodist Episcopal Church." They have three bishops, 300 ministers, and 21,237 members.

In 1828, a party in the Methodist Church, who thought themselves aggrieved by various regulations, seceded, and formed a new body under the title of the " Protestant Methodist Church." They have ceased to have bishops, and they admit lay representatives and local preachers to the government of the Church. They have 916 effective preachers, 70,018 members, and 103 home missionaries.

There are likewise the Welsh Calvinistic Methodists, with eighty-one ministers, and 3,950 members; the Primitive Methodist Church, with twelve ministers, and 1,100 members; and the Wesleyan Methodist Connection, with 310 ministers, and 23,000 members.

The different branches of the Methodist Church, taken in the aggregate, have twenty-five bishops, 366 presiding elders, 8,740 effective ministers, 1,593,794 members, and 1,197 home missionaries. Including "local preachers" and "superannuated ministers," many of whom preach a great deal, they have 22,209 ministers of all classes. They have 13,146 Sabbath-schools, and 129,885 teachers in such schools. From the foregoing statements it will be seen that the Evangelical denominations in the United States have a total of 42,359 churches, 29,430 ministers, 14,068 licentiates, 4,176,431 members, and a population of 17,762,000 under their influence.

CHAPTER IV.—*Non-Evangelical Churches in the United States.*

HE Roman Catholic Church is the most powerful. The Roman Catholic population may be estimated at 3,250,000. However, no one in America has any apprehensions of the progress of Popery. Popery is only a fraction amongst the elements of the United States, and it knows itself to be so. Many Romanists abjure their creed after reaching America, and the children in the next generation become Protestants in large numbers, partly through the influence of the common schools. The religious fanaticism which constitutes a large portion of the essence of Popery prospers under oppression and feeds on persecution, but has no power against genuine democracy. The complete religious liberty

which exists in America dissolves the war of
sects into a war of *abstract opinions*. The Romanists who have settled in America amount to
many millions; but, on comparing that number
with the number at present in the country, it is
found that millions are missing, and that education, toleration, and equality of rights, have
gradually and silently absorbed them.

About twenty-five years ago German Trans-
cendentalism made its appearance among the
Unitarian clergy, and has spread rapidly. Its
adherents are generally to be found among
shallow and misty thinkers. It promises to relieve its disciples from the burden of building
their faith on probabilities, however strong, and
to give them an infallible and intuitive knowledge of all that is essential in religion. I have
rarely met any Transcendentalists who were
acquainted with the philosophy of their belief
or the evidence on which it rests. They are
decidedly Pantheistic, and maintain that all re-
ligions are developments of the truth.

The "Christian Connection" is of purely
American origin, and boasts of having no human founder and no creed. They have 500
ministers, 35,000 members, and a population of

300,000 under their influence, by their own estimate.

The Universalists rose about 1760, and have increased considerably within the last fifty years. They teach that all punishment is in this life, and that all souls pass, after death, into a state of happiness. Many of their preachers are skilled in using all the weapons of sophistry. Their creed exercises no reforming influence, and is chiefly agreeable to the irreligious, the immoral, and all haters of Evangelical religion. They have 640 preachers, and about 500,000 of the population under their influence.

The New Jerusalem, or Swedenborgian Church, has about thirty-five ministers and 10,000 souls under its teaching. It holds many mystical vagaries, and its mode of interpreting Scripture is at variance with every principle of sound philosophy and exegesis.

The Rappists are a small sect of German Protestants located in the West, who practise a " community of goods."

The Shakers are a fanatical sect, of English origin, calling themselves the Millennial Church, and their communities, comprising about 7,500 souls, are principally to be found among the

E

mountains of New York and Massachusetts.
They hold that the Millennium has begun, and
that they are the only true Church possessing
the apostolic gifts.   They forbid marriage;
they maintain the doctrine of community of
goods, and the men and women live apart.
They are thrifty and industrious, but their religious observances resemble those of the Der-
vishes rather than those of a rational people.

The Mormons make few proselytes among
the Americans, and have been principally recruited from Britain.   They have been gradually driven westward, and now exist beyond
the Rocky Mountains as an isolated community
of about 50,000 souls.

The names of other fanaticisms have been
occasionally heard in England, but they are not
deserving of notice.   The fact is, that in America, when a new sect is started, it speedily attains the apogee of its notoriety, and runs into
some extravagance which ensures its speedy
downfal.   Altogether, the amount of outrageous error in the United States is small, and
a vast respect for true religion pervades the
moral atmosphere of the country.

CHAPTER V.—*New England.*

 WOULD be glad if my readers would now mentally separate the six New England States from the other sections of the Union, as the characteristics which they present are only to be found elsewhere in a faint degree. The influence of the Puritan settlers—" the sifted wheat" of England, as their descendants love to call them—is still felt in laws, customs, and religion. It has been, and is still, the fashion to ridicule those sturdy old colonists, and to represent them as sombre, covetous, hard, obstinate, and unloveable; indeed, the popular use of the epithet " Puritanical" reveals the estimation in which they and their compatriots were held. It is undeniable that the characters of some were tinged with fanaticism and even

with intolerance : obloquy and persecution have
a tendency to sour : there were hypocrites likewise among them, and men emulous of power ;
while others, with a misguided religious zeal,
attempted the unfortunate experiment of making men religious by legal enactments. But
we must make allowances for the temper of the
times, and also take into consideration the fact
that the first settlers left the restraints of law
behind them, and that nothing but an extreme
strictness could have built up an orderly and
moral community under such circumstances.

The Sabbath laws of New England, founded
on the old Puritan code, and sustained by the
will of the sovereign people, are unusually
strict, and remain a monument of the wisdom
of earlier legislators. Throughout New England business is suspended on the Lord's-day.
The ordinary trains cease to run. Even in
Springfield, the great centre of railway communication, quiet may be enjoyed. Pleasure ex-
cursions by railroad and steamer are unknown.
The stores are strictly closed. The day is devoted to religious worship and the enjoyment of
quiet social intercourse. A hush comes over
the busiest part of America, and even strangers

are compelled by the force of public opinion to recognize the sanctity of the day. These Sabbath laws have undoubtedly exercised a controlling and far-reaching influence in building up these noble States, and the people, however diverse their religious beliefs may be, still preserve them with jealous care in virtue of their physical necessity. New England, with its cities and busy villages, and smiling rural districts, presents to the view a Sabbath as unprofaned as can be witnessed in the Highlands of Scotland. Thus much for what judicious legislation can do.

With respect to the state of the Churches, one or two facts require brief notice. The Church in New England was virtually united to the State for many years. It was requisite for civil office that individuals should be Church members, so prevalent and strong was the public religious sentiment. The world demanded that the Church should meet it half-way : hence the latter was in danger of being corrupted. The doctrine prevailed to some extent that the Lord's Supper was a " means of grace," and not solely an ordinance whereby spiritual believers signify their living union with their Lord. As a " means of grace" all individuals of external morality were admitted to it, and hence every respectable man in the community was a Church member and eligible to office. It was under the influence of Jonathan Edwards that the tide of feeling on this subject began to turn; and in this cause for years he toiled and laboured, opposing the reception of any but " believers" into the Church. Now there is not a vestige of the old practice remaining, and none but those who profess themselves " regenerate," and walk, as far as man can see, consistently with their profession, are admitted to the Lord's Table. Upon these Church members devolve the important duties of choosing the minister and the elders and deacons. The efficiency and purity of the New England ministry cannot be a matter of surprise when we reflect that the ministers are chosen by those who, from the love of Christ, and with the spirit of Christ, unite to invite them, and promise to support them. Such a ministry, as a whole, is connected with the people by close and endearing associations. Nowhere have we seen ministers more beloved than in New England, where they are chosen and sustained by the people among whom they labour; they are superior to none, inferior to none; they are the trusted friends and counsellors of men alike of low and high degree; and they cannot sustain themselves, or retain their connection with any people, for one moment, after they cease to commend themselves to their consciences and affections. This ministry has a moral influence of incalculable power. This relation to the people is one in which the ministers of religion stand throughout the States; but its advantages are seen preeminently in New England, than which country there is none on earth where a Gospel ministry wields a more potent influence —an influence of a moral character solely, being exercised only on the conscience and understanding.

The theory prevailing in New England on this subject may be stated in few words, thus: —The Holy Spirit makes Christians, and the same Spirit, moving in these Christians, constitutes Churches, elects pastors, furnishes voluntarily the means of their support, and the same Spirit multiplies and confirms these communities. The State has nothing whatever to do with them, save as the religious sentiment, thus existing as a vast educational element, forces the recognition of God in all constitutions, enactments, proclamations, election sermons, legislative prayers, &c; and the establishment of laws to further and protect the worship of God in whatever manner the consciences of the people dictate. Christianity, therefore, stands on its own merits and potency as a social element, and advances only as it is made to commend itself to the conscious wants of the people, and as a regulating essential element of social condition. Christianity is there influential and respectable only as its teachings, its ministers, its professors, make it so; and men honour, love, and support those ministers only as, by patient teaching and Christian sincerity and faithfulness, they commend themselves unto the wants of humanity.

That Christianity is *influential* in New England is evident to the most unobservant stranger; for under its influence the Sabbath laws are retained and strengthened, principles of moderation and temperance prevail, and the Government, deferring to the public religious sentiment by an annual proclamation, couched often in terms that would not bring discredit upon the pulpit, appoints a solemn fast, a day of national humiliation, which is observed like the Sabbath, and in the glowing autumn a day of thanksgiving for the mercies of the harvest. That Christianity is *respectable* is proved by the great number of wealthy and influential persons who profess it, and, by a certain amount of hypocrisy, that homage which vice renders to virtue.

In Boston, and the other large cities, we can only judge of the influence of religion by externals. The aspect of Boston is orderly; intoxicated persons are rarely to be seen in the streets; and that town of nearly 200,000 inhabitants is so quiet at night that a respectable female may walk unattended along any of the streets. Races are not known; and, whatever may be the tendency among the lowest of the population to prize-fighting, professional gambling at gambling-houses, cock-fighting, &c, it is prevented from development by the strong arm of the law. The Sabbath in Boston itself is rigidly observed. The churches are all crowded; the stores are closed so completely that a stranger finds himself baffled in the attempt to obtain even a glass of soda-water; the

still waters of the harbour are undisturbed by
the keel of a single steamer, and no railroad
whistle pierces the air. In fact, Boston city
wears on the Sabbath what may justly be called
a Puritanical aspect. *Outside* the town, along
the roads leading to the numerous suburban
villages, numbers of vehicles are to be seen,
and the practice of driving on Sunday is on the
increase in that locality. What is true of Boston on the Sabbath is true of all the New England cities; and in the inland towns, which are
free from the vitiating influences of a foreign
Roman Catholic population, the decorum is
even more apparent. The country districts are,
however, the most completely under the religious or Puritan influence, and to them the
New Englanders point with pride, as to a part
of the world which is unequalled for its moral
beauty. In them religion displays itself as the
most powerful of all social elements. There it
has planted the church, the college, and the
school; it has given free institutions and free
speech; it has trained up a noble population of
freemen, religious, moral, intelligent, and industrious, dwelling in happy homes, that are
the centres of light and love, and which are

found only in a land where the Bible is honoured, and where the Sabbath is observed.
These districts present the remarkable spectacle
of a population engaged in peaceful pastoral
pursuits, without being dulled by them, tilling
the ground which their fathers have tilled before
them, educating their children in the fear of
God, their sons rising to the highest positions
in the country, or carrying to the Far West the
leaven of religion and morality. Virtue, sobriety, industry, reverence for the Sabbath, and
love of order, characterize the country population throughout these six States. The people
are educated and enlightened, and every man,
when he casts his vote, can tell you exactly on
what grounds he supports a candidate. Bun-
yan's " Pilgrim's Progress," Edwards' works,
and some standard volumes of theology, are to
be found in almost the humblest library, and
the people are ready to discuss any point of
theology with intelligence.

Having mentioned the strict observance of the
Sabbath in the cities, I may describe a Sabbath
in a New England village ; and a description of
any one part, I can say from a somewhat extended experience, is descriptive of the whole.

I take the loveliest village in that surpassingly
fair portion of America. It is a village of
5,000 people, built on a collection of knolls,
rising from park-like meadows, through which
flow the bright waters of the rushing Connecticut. Beyond the meadows picturesque hills
form an amphitheatre, enclosing this gem of
Massachusetts, and in whichever direction the
eye of the gazer turns, it is satiated with bright
visions of material beauty. The village itself
consists of a collection of lanes shaded by ave-
nues of gigantic weeping elms, and along these
lanes are erected detached cottages, embosomed
in roses and vines. It dates from an early period of the seventeenth century, and some of
the families are descended from those which
landed on Plymouth Rock. There are five
churches: two Congregational, one Episcopalian, one Baptist, and one Methodist. Their
ministers all live in harmony, and engage together in union prayer-meetings. There is no
inn or tavern where liquor is sold in the place,
and not one policeman or gaol is required for
the extensive district. Although it appears to
slumber peacefully under the shade of its huge
elms, it is not deficient in New England enter-

prise, and is busy up to seven o'clock on Saturday evening. At that hour business ceases; and some families still keep up the old Puritan custom, which scarcely prevails beyond the Connecticut Valley, of commencing the Sabbath at six o'clock on Saturday evening by the putting away of all secular employments and books.

The Sabbath morning dawns, and the good people are up betimes, to see that their children's lessons are well prepared, and to despatch them to the Sabbath-school; for in New England children and young people of all classes and ages attend school, and very frequently the link is only broken by marriage. The Sabbath-school bell rings, and the trampling of many feet is heard; after which there is a profound stillness, broken only by the music of the oriole and the rustle of the humming-bird among the flowers. The sun's rays quiver through the thick trees and dance upon the bright green grass, the cattle repose lazily in the meadows, the mountain shadows lie over the landscape, and man, for once, does not deface what God has made so beautiful. At ten the bell for " meeting" rings, and shortly after

nearly the whole population is seen moving to
the respective churches, while rude country
vehicles, well laden with human freights, pour
in along the different lanes. The children who,
before this hour, have returned from school,
invariably accompany their parents, and generally walk according to age, the youngest first,
each with bible and hymn-book in hand, and
the parents bring up the rear. The assembling
of the congregations is a beautiful sight: there
is age with its venerable aspect and snowy
hair; childhood and youth in their grace and
beauty; manhood in its summer prime; whole
families, grandparents and grandchildren, going
up to the house of God as those that keep holi-
day. Every church in that fair village is
filled; for all the people are church-goers.
After the service has commenced, all is unbroken silence again; even the horses which
bring the country people in, and which are
tethered outside the churches, to the number of
seventy or eighty, to posts placed there for the
purpose, behave with remarkable propriety.
Service is over at half-past twelve; at one Sabbath-school recommences; and at two service
is held again; at four the lanes are again

thronged with people and wagons, and the families assemble for religious instruction in their several houses according to good old custom, and the roads are silent again; at seven " Concerts for Prayer" are held in the lecture-rooms of the different churches, those on the first Sunday in each month being invariably for the purpose of prayer for missions and for the communication of missionary information. This last service being over, the people stroll along the lanes, relations visit each other, and families, in the summer evenings, sit on the doorsteps of the houses, enjoying a twilight lighted by the fitful sparkle of the fireflies, and in the winter assemble round blazing log-fires. It is hardly too much to say that these Sabbaths do more than anything else to cement those bonds of family affection which we have never seen stronger than in New England; to make home a charmed spot, ever fresh and ever fragrant; and to keep in active exercise those holy affections that make up the purest of life's enjoyments, and smooth so many of life's sorrows. Such is the external influence of religion in the country districts of New England. Her fairest village is a type, not an exceptional case, as all

who know her will testify. I have painted no
Utopian scene. It is the wide-spread influence
of religion which has made New England, with
her severe climate and her barren soil, the most
prosperous portion of the Union; which has
produced her well-regulated families, her virtuous sons and virtuous daughters, and which
renders so many of her people contented with
the peaceful pursuits which they follow, each
in his and her own sphere moving silently but
surely to the grand result of all virtuous actions, the good of the whole. It is New England families, carrying their religion with them,
who have leavened the mighty West, and have
planted the Church, the School—yes, and the
Sabbath, too—on its vast prairies. It has been
the fashion to sneer at this nation of " Psalm-
singers ;" but the order-loving and moral population of New England is the best answer to the
taunt, and is the noblest monument to the
worth of the Puritan character. I wish I could
stop here, and that truth would permit me to
leave the picture as it is; but there are dis-
figuring shadows behind, and an impartial inspection will not fail to discover to us " the
trail of the serpent."

Such are the bright aspects of religion in
New England. In no country is its influence
more potent, and there are no spots of earth
where I would more willingly linger in thought
than among the mountains of New Hampshire
and Vermont and the villages of Maine and
Massachusetts. But, while New England is a
monument of what religion has power to do for
our fallen humanity, in elevating its social and
moral condition, truth compels me to add that
one or two of the cities, decorous as are their
externals, have been the great *foci* of error, the
hotbeds in which most of the *isms* which have
flourished for a longer or shorter period in the
North and West have been successfully raised.
It is a singular thing that the New England
mind, so highly educated, so intellectual, and so
analytical, should foster, if not create, some of
the wildest extravagances which exist and some
of the most dangerous errors which have ever
been evolved from the book of truth—extravagances which are asserting their sway over
thousands in America, bewildering the intellect
and perverting the heart; and errors which,
multiplied a thousandfold by the press, and
gilded by the splendour of intellect and genius,

F

are pouring their pernicious streams wherever
the English language is spoken.

The distinctions between what is termed
" orthodoxy," i. e. Evangelical truth, and the
various forms of error, are very marked. Every
man has opinions of some kind or other on the
subject of religion. Complete indifference is
rarely to be met with in New England. A
man's religious opinions are as patent among
his acquaintances as his business or profession.
Religion is not a subject tabooed either in literary, fashionable, or mercantile circles. Every
man discusses it and declares his opinions upon
it; but the line which separates truth from
error is rigidly adhered to, and the New England Churches exercise a zealous guardianship
over faith. A minister may take up such notions on faith and the atonement as are held by
the extreme section of the Broad Church party,
but it is at the penalty of dismission from his
charge; or a Church member may adopt notions
respecting the Divinity of our Lord contrary to
the articles of faith, but it is at the risk of ex-
communication.

Unitarianism, since 1780, has extensively
prevailed in Boston, Worcester, Springfield,

and a few other of the New England cities.
They have 360 churches, most of which are in
Massachusetts. Unitarianism dates from the
time when Edwards, Whitefield, and Stoddard
made their attacks upon men's hopes of heaven.
Some errors into which the promoters of the
" Great Revival" of that period fell accelerated
the secession; but Unitarianism grew out of a
dislike to the practice of requiring evidence of
piety in candidates for admission to the Churches.
The Unitarians hold opinions varying from Ari-
anism to Socinianism regarding the divinity of
our Lord. Some of them are of stern morality;
others are of a large faith and a comprehensive
charity; most practise an extended philanthropy.
A large part of the wealth of Eastern Massachusetts is in their hands; Boston is their
stronghold, and they include within their pale
much of the literary ability of that polished
capital.

The upper classes in Boston are mainly Unitarian. The churches are numerous and hand-
some, the pulpit singularly able, the music superior, and the congregations philanthropic.
Among many of the Unitarians there is a sedu-
lous attention to the externals of religion; at-

tendance twice a-day at church, a decent observance of the Sabbath, liberal support furnished
to ministers, and, in many families, daily prayer
and unbounded munificence characterize them.
The architecture of the churches, the crowded
congregations, the beautiful language employed
in prayer and preaching, and the influence of
exquisite taste pervading the worship, cannot
fail to impress a stranger. But all is cold and
lifeless. The prayers, if such they can be
called, consist of sublime ascriptions of adoration, thanksgivings for wealth, for liberty, for
moral and intellectual elevation, and eloquent
aspirations after abstract virtue and such per-
fection as will enable man to stand before his
Creator; but the name of Him by whom alone
the guilty can approach God is wanting. The
pulpit is equally eloquent. The fire of Chan-
ning's glowing periods still burns on many lips;
every human element is brought into requisi-
tion which can charm the intellect or elevate the
soul. Whether Divine goodness be the theme,
the virtues of the Redeemer, the hatefulness of
vice, the beauty of virtue, the poetry of Isaiah,
or the metaphysics of Paul, the subject is treated
with all the force of which human thought is

capable, and decked with all the graces which can be borrowed from poetry, literature, or art. No expense is spared by the wealthy congregations to procure a minister of the highest intellectual attainments, who shall possess the power to make the Sabbath sermon the richest intellectual feast of the week; and the Unitarian pulpit boasts at the present time of some of the profoundest scholars and most accomplished orators in America.

A religion which lowers Divinity and raises humanity, and professes to carry men to heaven on the shoulders of a pure morality; which ignores the " vulgar" questions of sin and punishment, and tramples upon the doctrine of human depravity; which stimulates moral self-complacency and intellectual pride, is very certain to find favour where the deification of intellect is so common, and where the preaching of Calvinistic doctrine prevails. In many of the Unitarian churches the service is altogether unwritten; but in the old King's Chapel at Boston, and some others, the Liturgy of the Church of England, expurgated of all passages which infringe upon the Unitarian creed, is regularly read.

Harvard College, the Cambridge of America, one of the very few colleges in the country not under Evangelical influence, is one of the chief supports of Unitarianism. Within its walls some of the noblest and most gifted youth of America have become proselytised to a creed so congenial to human pride. Around it are grouped, in a brilliant galaxy, some of the most gifted men in the country—Longfellow, Lowell, Sparks, Peirce, Dana, Holmes, and others—men who shed their lustre upon the age in which they live. Not far off, too, is Emerson, that eloquent mystic, who is ever leading the young and ardent into the quagmire of his own doubts and the darkness of his own conceits. All these brilliant literary men are Unitarians, belonging generally to the Transcendental school of which Emerson is the acknowledged leader. Neither is religion an exploded subject among these luminaries. As one of the greatest of moral and intellectual questions, it is conti-- nually discussed at the frequent reunions; and the foundations of faith 'meet with but scant courtesy from the elegant contempt of Long-fellow, the brilliant wit of Lowell, and the subtle analysis of Peirce or Horsford. It takes its stand with other questions, to be disposed of with them by the rules of historic credibility and the laws of reason. The intellectual and social fascinations of these gifted literary men, as may be expected, are ever propagating Unitarian error, which, as from a great centre, radiates from Boston and its neighbourhood.

Still, not all the eloquence of the pulpit, nor all the charms which genius and intellect throw round error, nor the adaptation of its doctrines to the pride of the human heart, can succeed in sustaining Unitarianism in the position in New England which it formerly occupied. The heart seeks for more in religion than intellectual abstractions, and our smitten humanity cries out for a living Saviour, who shall have at once the nature to sympathize with our wants and the power to relieve them, and can only be satisfied with the knowledge of the High Priest who is passed into the heavens—Jesus, the Son of God. Hence in a large section of the Unitarian body there is a continual verging towards orthodoxy. In some few instances whole congregations have abandoned their errors; and during the past summer Mr. Coolidge, one of the leading preachers in Boston, publicly re-

nounced Unitarianism in one of the most solemn
and beautiful addresses which I ever perused.
There is such a strong and visible movement
towards "orthodoxy," that it is probable another
thirty years will witness the complete extinction of the present mongrel species of Unitarianism in many districts in its favour, and the
passing of other congregations into grosser
forms of error.

At Boston there is a preacher of great talent
and captivating manner, who has the distinction
mentioned in Revelations, of " adding unto the
prophecy of this book." He only takes *away*
therefrom, in common with many of his contem-
poraries. His followers are named Parkerites.
I have not space to enter into a detail of his
opinions. He holds in part the ultra-Unitarian
form of error; he is in part a Pantheist; he
holds that all truth-loving, virtuous men, are
inspired; and in the churches of his followers
the ministers will read in " the Gospel according to St. Mark" at the morning service, and
" the Gospel according to Theodore Parker" in
the evening. His opinions have infected some
of the highly intellectual men and women of
New England. He is preeminently distin-

guished by his views on the subject of marriage.
He holds that it is merely a temporary contract,
and that want of congeniality of tastes, as well
as incompatibility of temper, are sufficient
grounds for a divorce; and his views on this
point are spreading among the youthful, and
perhaps especially among the female portion of
the community. Some of the practical appli-
cations of his principles on this subject would
be ludicrous, if they were not too sad. A husband, a few weeks after a hasty marriage, finds
that his wife has no love for poetry; an extravagant wife finds that her husband is not disposed to allow her money wherewith to pur-
chase the twenty-one new and fashionable dresses
which are a *sine quâ non* for the indispensable
three weeks' trip to Newport or Saratoga; and
in both these instances a speedy legal release is
obtained, leaving each individual free to try the
experiment of marriage over again, very possibly with the same result. At the present
time there are 2,000 persons residing tempo-
rarily in Indiana and Illinois, where the law of
divorce is very lax, to obtain freedom from ma-
trimonial shackles.

I pass on to a brief notice of Spiritualism, the

indigenous growth of Germany transplanted to
New England. A few years ago there was a
general mania for forming circles round tables,
which, under these circumstances, were supposed to be capable of such prodigies as stolid
furniture had never before been guilty of. The
timid were alarmed; the credulous were bewil-
dered; the clergy shook their heads; the would-
be *savans* talked mysteriously of electrical
agency; a few persons whose intellects were
tottering were hurried prematurely into lunatic
asylums; the men of practical science poured
contempt on the whole; and, after a season or
two, the mania was forgotten in England.

Not so in America. Spiritualism has there
grown into a creed, and demands observation
and investigation as such, challenging the four
most learned professors of the natural sciences
in the States to pronounce it an imposture, after
prolonged analysis, which to all intents ánd
purposes they failed to do. The number of professed spiritualists is estimated at from 650,000
to 2,000,000. They are to be found in all classes,
and some of them are regular attendants on
orthodox worship. The more advanced among
them receive Spiritualism as a religious belief,

and take as the latest of Divine revelations the
" Great Harmonia" and " Penetralia," the works
of a man who is held in abhorrence by all that
is virtuous and good. They are to be found in
the best-educated circles; and, if it were desirable, we could mention the names of several
men of eminence in the scientific and literary
world who belong to them. They have their
affiliated societies, their newspapers, and their
literature. They are ever increasing both in
numbers and extravagances, and are one of the
most monstrous developments of the present
age.

It would be foreign to my present purpose to
enter into the *minutiæ* of Spiritualism. A celebrated trance medium, who has recently re-
canted his errors, describes it as " partly imposture, partly credulity, and partly diabolism,"
and it is my belief that he is entirely right.
There are few towns in New England which
have not their spiritual circles, which meet two
or three times a week to carry on their real or
imaginary intercourse with the spirits of the
departed, with angels in heaven and demons in
hell. We do not speak of professional spiritualists, but of ladies and gentlemen who are

trance mediums, writing mediums, and speaking mediums, who meet with all the paraphernalia which a love of the Satanic or credulity can suggest, to practise a worse than ancient witchcraft. To these circles men have the audacity to summon Michael and Gabriel, as well as the Archfiend himself; the place of torment gives up its tortured inmates, and heaven the spirits of the departed blest. Abraham and Moses, Herod and Judas, come alike from some scene of material bliss to gainsay the assertions of " priestcraft." Or, in less daring circles, Cæsar continues his commentaries and Shakespeare his plays; Bacon produces an amended system of philosophy, and Scott another novel. These fictitious works are printed, published, sold, and admired; but, seriously, if the decay of genius in another life is so great as these works represent, its worshippers had better rest satisfied with its efforts in this. There are other circles where things future are revealed, where departed spirits communicate messages of love to their loved ones, and the veiled secrets of another life are disclosed. It would not be wise to intrench upon the mysteries of these unhallowed reunions, or to speak of the further extremes into which their votaries run; the statistics of the lunatic asylums show to what goal this commingling of the real and the unreal is continually carrying the victims of the desire to know what God has concealed.

But there are other Spiritualists who nourish their faith in the quiet of their hearts and homes, who are their own " mediums " of communication with the unseen. These are the bereaved ones who nightly solace themselves with supposed communion with the spirits of their departed ones, and feed with pitiable avidity on their accounts of the spirit land, and seek their advice on every step which they take in life. I have heard such persons narrate such interviews with painful pleasure and painful minuteness, as if they felt that the heart-hunger which death ever leaves were in great measure appeased by them. But, from all that I have ever heard, I can only say, with Mrs. Stowe, that the spirits who have spoken must be in a very different heaven from that of Paul or John, for there is no echo of the new song. If the " sanctities of heaven," our beautiful and glorified ones, are to stoop lower than the level of their cast-off bodies to rap, and juggle, and squeak, and perform mountebank tricks with tables and chairs, and repeat in dreary sameness things which we could say better for ourselves, sadly and soberly I say that, if this be communion with the dead, it is best to be without it; and, if this be the immortality of which our world-worn spirits dream, annihilation would be infinitely preferable. I shall not lay before my readers any of the practice of Spiritualism. " Ignorance," on this subject, " is bliss." But I have said enough to show that, among the most educated people in the world, there exists a system which, if statistics are to be relied upon, is holding in a terrible moral captivity at least 650,000 persons—a system which, if it is " credulity and imposture" only, is the worst of modern extravagances; but, if it is " diabolism" also, is the worst of modern heresies. It is ever adding to its monstrosities and the number of its adherents, and is the greatest disgrace of New England, bringing a slur upon the influence of religion, and giving rise to serious doubts as to the efficiency of the educational system.

I have not done with the heresies and fanaticisms of New England. It may surprise some persons to find Abolitionism among the latter. In England there is a very general feeling against slavery—American slavery especially—which is regarded by many as "*the sum of all villanies.*" And the only party in the States which is supposed to have any sincere abhorrence of the system, or any definite plan for its extinction, excites a sympathy on this side of the Atlantic, which it is very far from deserving, and is given, I am persuaded, in exact proportion to the ignorance of the sympathisers as to the character and position of the Abolitionists. I shall devote rather more space to a notice of this party than its numerical importance may seem to warrant. Its tendencies are closely connected with the religion or the irreligion of New England; and the sympathy which is evinced towards it by a portion of the religious public in England is a grievance which the Christians of America feel rather keenly. I am particularly anxious not to be misunderstood in my subsequent observations. I am no apologist for slavery, and abhor it in common with all other tyrannies; but as long as it is as profitable in the sugar and cotton growing S ates as it is now, there is little expectation or hope of its extinction. I fear much that it will endure, adding to the dark catalogue of human wrong, until the approach of our world's great Liberator, who, in assuming the crown of universal empire, shall bid the oppressed go free and break every yoke.

" Slavery is an evil; the abolition of it would be a good; therefore, the Abolitionists must be a very good set of people." This is a favourite English syllogism, the truth of which is not apparent.

A certain party in New England, of a somewhat peculiar idiosyncrasy, being disgusted with the existing order of things, and with the federal connection subsisting between such opposite sections of the Union as North and South, established an association, which has for its objects the severance of this tie, or the complete and immediate abolition of slavery, without any compensation to the slaveholders for the loss of their human property. It is but justice to say, that the originator of this society, William Lloyd Garrison, is a man of undoubted philanthropy, and has on several occasions proved his fidelity to his principles. However, whatever the original objects of this association were, it has become a Cave of Adullam, in which the discon-

tented factious spirits of the North find a refuge, and its annual convention takes the rank
of a political caucus of the lowest grade, from
which the slave and his interests are almost entirely banished. The platform of the Abolitionists is quite unique. " Disunion, Revolution, and Abolition !" They abjure the Constitution ; do not vote at elections ; and are ineli-
gible for any political offices. They are a political under the pretext of being a philanthropic
society. They print and circulate, openly in the
North, and clandestinely in the South, large
numbers of inflammatory tracts, written by men
and women of undoubted ability. They have
paid agents, who are actively employed in
" stumping" the North-Western States, and in
circulating tracts among the slaves, also in providing the means of transit for those who are
not afraid to incur the risk of bloodhounds'
fangs, ear-slitting, beating, branding, and the
other concomitants of an unsuccessful attempt
to escape. Occasionally the zeal of some of the
last-mentioned agents is in advance of their dis-
cretion, and " tarring and feathering," with " a
ride on a rail" out of the district in which the
offence has been committed, is often their fate

G

after a brief trial by lynch law. I cannot extol
their consistency as much as their misguided
zeal; for some of the same men who will risk their
lives for the slave, by defying the popular sentiment in the South, are the first to oppose any
cession of social or political privileges to the free
negro in the North. They are vehemently opposed to the Christian Anti-Slavery Society, of
which the late lamented Mr. Tyng, Dr. Cheever,
and Henry Ward Beecher were the ornaments,
and it comes under their annual maledictions at
their annual conference. I give some space to
a mention of this society, because much surprise
is felt in England that Christians in America
who are opposed to slavery should stand aloof
from it, and because it is an important and con-
spicuous New England development. I will
not dwell upon what we believe to be the chi-
merical nature of its aims, as far as slavery is
concerned, but upon the definite war which it
wages against revealed religion or " orthodoxy,"
and a brief account of its annual convention will
show its real nature more forcibly than anything
else to English minds. I vouch for the accu-
racy of the report, but frankly confess that this
is only giving a portion of the truth, for I could

not deform these pages with the impiety which is breathed from an Abolitionist platform. My readers must bear in mind that this is a description of the grand annual convention of an association which has for its nominal object the enfranchisement of four millions of slaves, and which excites a good deal of sympathy among English Christians.

The announcement that the Abolitionist Convention would meet in Boston attracted a concourse of the members of the society, who met for two successive days in a dark, dingy old theatre hired for the purpose. The assembly, even for America, was a curious one, and I doubt whether any other object could have collected into one room 800 people whose external characteristics were so very remarkable. The gentlemen generally wore very long beards, and very long hair, divided in the middle, and frequently trained into elaborate ringlets, which fell over the shoulders. Many of them possessed the prefix of *Reverend*. The ladies were singularly ill-favoured, and all had long ago discarded any pretensions to youth or beauty. They had a uniform angularity of visage, and a bold masculine look, suggestive of the epithet

" strong-minded," a term of opprobrium in America. In a country where so much attention is paid to dress, it was worthy of note that the habiliments of all were in a style now obsolete; that the bonnets actually did cover the face, and that the skirts, both as to length and circumference, were the very reverse of the prevailing fashion. Five Bloomers, in a costume which neither youth nor beauty could have rendered picturesque, owing to the economy displayed in its arrangement, failed to attract any attention. Many of these ladies, including the Bloomers, belonged to the Woman's Right Society, and contended for a perfect equality with the " lords of creation." I never witnessed a more unsightly assemblage.

The proceedings commenced with an invocation of universal Deity on behalf of universal humanity, especially of the Abolitionist portion of it in convention assembled. Garrison was the first speaker. He animadverted in very strong language on the attitude of the orthodox Churches. He said that they had been experimenting with orthodoxy for two centuries, and, though it was a failure, America was bound by it hand and foot. He was violent, though not

profane in his language, but it was too evident
that his *animus* was against true religion.
Wendell Phillips, whose name is well known
in England, was the next speaker. His talent
is great, and his oratory takes a very high place
in America. I believe him to possess, in common with Garrison, the merit of sincerity, and
I could hear him with gratification on any other
subject. He abused religion, hurled maledictions against the Constitution and the Churches,
declared that his soul was under no trammels,
argued in favour of disunion, stated that the
Union was a husk to be puffed away for its
worthlessness, and that the watchword of his
followers must be " Ready for Revolution!"
Anecdote, tirade, fact, joke, fancy, sarcasm, wit,
and argument, mingled in a flowing, and to the
audience a captivating, stream. He stigmatised
Washington and Jesus Christ as traitors to humanity; the one as the author of the Constitution, the other of the New Testament, both of
which encourage slavery; after which he proceeded to denounce Beecher and Cheever, the
senators from Massachusetts, and the Republican party, as the most dangerous enemies of
the Abolitionists, who are at war with the Go-

vernment, the pulpit, and the other institutions
which enslave men, body and soul. He said
that when the ship of State was launched, some
years ago, the Devil hovered over Charleston
and let fall a cotton seed, which speedily anni-
hilated the principles of liberty and turned the
empire into a vast cotton bag. One by one all
the political and religious institutions of this
country had gone over to the slave power, and
now the Abolitionists were left alone. He wanted
something to meet this march of despotism—a
deeply-seated prejudice and enmity such as animated Protestants and Catholics in old times,
so that when they met they would fly at each
other's throats. His peroration, which was
vociferously applauded, was in these words:
" I wish to have such an enmity to slavery that
when I ' shuffle off this mortal coil,' the chemist,
on subjecting my frame to ultimate analysis,
shall find as the sole residue *curses* for South
Carolina." The slave and his condition were
merely alluded to incidentally. The burden of
the speech was an attack on orthodoxy and the
Republican party. Some resolutions were read
condemnatory of the Republican party, couched
in outrageous phraseology, alluding by name to

the noble Charles Sumner. A lady in full
Bloomer costume spoke to them first at the
evening session, declaring that if there were an
orthodox hell Charles Sumner would be there.
She declared that she was bold enough to deny
that creation of credulity and priestcraft, named
the Deity, and proceeded in a strain of profanity
and infidelity never so repulsive as when coming
from a woman's lips. The next speaker was
Matthew Hull, who had been engaged for twelve
years in stumping the North-Western States
for the Abolition cause. He was hard-featured
and cunning-looking, yet had a dash of cheeri-
ness in his face and manner, which secured him
the good will of the audience. He spoke in a
high-pitched, rapid, and stentorian voice, and,
although a Virginian, with an inimitable nasal
twang, his speech was an admirable specimen
of stump oratory—noisy claptrap, rough wit,
outrageous declamation, indescribable vehe-
mence, and universal humbug. He frequently
forgot that he was in the American Athens,
for he indulged in a superabundance of· Western slang which would have been repulsive
to any other audience. He was generally
very amusing, occasionally very forcible, often

very profane. After sketching his life, his arrest in a Methodist chapel while speaking on Wesley's words, " Slavery is the sum of all villanies," his escape from gaol, and subsequent career, he gave a vivid description of the way in which the religion of a slave was used by the auctioneers to enhance his price. " Ah," he said, truthfully but irreverently, " Christ says all who keep his commandments are his brethren —the slaveholder sells Christ's brethren ; He says the Holy Ghost dwells in his people—the slaveholder sells the temple of the Holy Ghost ; He says his people are one with him—then the slaveholder sells Christ himself. Judas was a gentleman compared with the slaveowner. I love Judas ! I love Judas ! he was a man of some feeling and conscience ; he will be in the third heaven, and the slaveholder in the lowest hell, for he sells Divinity twenty times over, and has not the grace to repent and hang himself." This was loudly applauded ; the sympathies of the audience were evidently enlisted in favour of Judas.

Mr. Parker Pilsbury spoke next. He began by a malignant attack upon " orthodoxy," particularly as represented by the Rev. Dudley

Tyng and Dr. Cheever. He was quiet in his manner, elegant in his diction, and grave and severe in his remarks. He declared himself an infidel, professed to be at war with all creeds and governments, and wished to punish the slavery party in this world, as he had no terrors of orthodox perdition in the next to shake over their heads. He declared eternal war against all who live south of " Mason and Dixon's line," and boasted, in the words of a better man, that the men of Massachusetts would never meet the men of South Carolina except upon the battle-field. He described Charles Sumner as misguided, timorous, weak, and wicked; the author of the triumph of slavery; and stigmatised President Buchanan as the " personification of Border-Ruffianism, the mystery of Iniquity, and the son of Perdition."

One coloured man addressed the Convention in a truly eloquent speech, in which he denounced the Supreme Court of the United States, and that now celebrated decision of Chief Justice Taney, that " *a coloured man has no rights which a white man is bound to respect.*" The spirit of malignity and hate with which he spoke seemed almost to sit appropriately on one who belonged to a race possessing neither rights nor privileges, no liberty, no country, and no home.

The Convention remained two days in session, and three-and-twenty speeches were made, full of daring impiety, breathing threatenings and slaughter against man, and railing at " the throne of God, and him that sitteth thereon." I have only ventured to give some of the most harmless specimens of the style of the orators, and I forbear making any comment upon them. Of the meeting I will only say, to its credit, that there was no mawkish, maudlin cant about humanity and philanthropy. The slave was not made the stalking-horse of the vituperations which were not hurled against the South half so much as at the Republican party and the orthodox Churches. The speakers characterized the latter as " mean, base, bad-hearted, wicked, contemptible, and cowardly." They spoke of ministers " holding palavers, and guzzling and chuckling over their communion wine." The denunciations of the Churches seemed to afford the keenest satisfaction to the audience, although the speakers did not propose any substitute for their systematic rascality. It appeared a sin-

gular paradox, that people who proclaimed their
disbelief in eternal perdition should continually
invoke it on all who differed from them. I
think that English sympathy would hardly be
freely given to persons who on any public platform would ventilate sentiments so vicious in
language so objectionable.

It must not be for a moment supposed that
Mrs. Stowe, Henry Ward Beecher, and Dr.
Cheever, are identified with these political Abolitionists. They work through evil report and
good report, but more generally the former,
against the iniquity of slavery; but while no
tongues more eloquent or pens more able are
employed in the cause, they and their friends are
deficient in that organization and publicity of action which renders the Abolitionists so notorious.

These extravagances, which have their chief
development in the New England States, are
much to be deplored; yet we must be slow to
put any beyond the pale of our charity on
whom God's sun shines and his rains descend.
The evil is often glaring; the good works noise-
lessly, but surely. If I have at all exaggerated
the evil, or placed it in too strong a light, it is
with the intention of showing the strength and

power of truth. In New England true religion
is the prevailing influence felt from the Government downwards. Unitarianism is on the de-
cline, and modifies its doctrines in obedience to
the prevailing religious sentiment. The various
fanatical sects which arise take for a time a
glaring position before the public eye, and then
wither and decay. Infidelity displays a bold
front, especially on Abolitionist platforms; but
it is less rife than elsewhere. While the Scriptures are received, by the great majority, as the
standards of moral truth and right, while the
Sabbath is observed, while what may be termed
a religious influence pervades the country, and
above all while the Churches, the depositories
of truth, are pure in doctrine and practice—although there may be much which appears dark
there is more, far more, to cause thankfulness
and hope. I believe that the New England
States are the most moral, perhaps the most
religious portion of the world, and that in the
hearts of their people the love of their sacred
hereditary faith is equally strong with their
attachment to the undying principles of democratic liberty—the bequest, in each instance,
of their honoured Puritan ancestors.

CHAPTER VII.—*The Southern States and
Slavery.*

N English minds the " South" is less
associated with its varied beauties,
its forests of almost tropical vege-
tation, the fragrance of its orange
groves, and the rich scent of its blossoming
magnolias, its many-tinted flowers, and scarlet-
winged flamingoes, and all the rich productions
of its sunny climate, than with the one great
curse of SLAVERY with which all things are
interwoven. It is the existence of this foul
blot on Christianity, often ignorantly charged
upon the whole of America, which has done
more than anything else to produce sceptical
feelings in many minds as to the reality of the
" Great Awakening;" and that religion and
Slavery can coexist in the South is very frequently doubted. I shall probably be misun-

derstood in the subsequent remarks, partly in consequence of a prejudice, by no means altogether reprehensible, against everything connected with the Slave States, and partly in consequence of a very general want of information as to their social and religious economy. I have frequently met well-educated persons who have asked questions based upon the idea that Slavery exists in New York and New England; and the generality of English people are so totally ignorant of the constitution of the United States that they suppose that Slavery could be instantaneously abolished by Act of Congress. In point of fact, Congress has no more power to interfere with Slavery in any State than the Russian Government has to prohibit Sunday trading in England; and to charge the iniquities of the system upon the Northern States is as absurd as it would be to make England responsible for the tyrannies practised in Naples. Each State has sovereign power as far as its internal arrangements are concerned, and it rests with each Slave State, and with no other authority in the Republic, to abolish Slavery within its own limits. The knowledge which most persons have of the South is taken

from the writings of Mrs. Beecher Stowe; and
though I am perfectly ready to testify to the
faithfulness of her brilliant word-paintings, as
far as my observation has extended, knowledge
so derived can only be considered very partial,
and as hardly affording sufficient *data* on which
to found an argument.

It is necessary to offer some remarks on slavery, as religion in the South is intimately connected with it. The most favourable view
shows it to be very injurious to true religion.
It fosters an unfeeling, arrogant, and proud
spirit in the master, and leads to servility and
deceitfulness, with their kindred vices, in the
slave. It likewise acts as a serious obstacle to
the working of the voluntary system, first by
creating two classes who can rarely hear the
truth of God in each other's presence, owing to
the extreme reluctance which slaves feel to
come into contact with persons to whom they
are placed in ignoble subjection. Secondly, it
creates a state of society unfavourable to the
providing the means of grace for all. The few
wealthy proprietors of a district will frequently
unite in supporting a church in some central
point which is easy of access with their horses

and carriages, but which is quite out of the reach of the hundreds or thousands of their dependents. In the country districts, where the owners are opposed to religion, the Gospel reaches the slaves with great difficulty and very irregularly, and then principally by the itinerating agencies of the Methodists. Thirdly, an unjust legislation in ten of the Slave States has forbidden the teaching of the slaves to read; so that all their religious knowledge must be derived from the lips of the living teacher, from whose ministrations they are frequently cut off. There is an impression prevailing in England that the slaveholders are divided into two classes; brutal, hateful *Legrees,* and amiable, visionary *St. Clairs.* From a knowledge of the subject, derived partly from actual observation and partly from reliable sources, I should say that those men in whose natures cruelty is inherrent can practise it especially in the South-Western States with less restraint than in England; and that in instances where gross barbarity can be clearly proved against the owner or overseer, punishment is very uncertain, from the leaning which judge and jury have to the white man, and the fact that the only evidence

which could generally be produced in proof of
the cruelty is that of a slave, which is inadmis-
sible in a court of justice. I believe, however,
that instances of wanton cruelty are far less
frequent than many people suppose; for the
majority of the slaveowners are as accurate in
their calculations of profit and loss as other
people; and apart from any humanitarian considerations, mercenary motives only are sufficient to protect the slave from personal injury,
and to procure for him wholesome food, warm
clothing in winter, sufficient rest, and the best
medical care, especially when able-bodied young
men are selling at £250 apiece. Owing to various circumstances, many of the estates in the
extreme South are passing out of the hands of
their old feudal proprietors, who have an hereditary love for the people on their properties,
into those of mere mercenary traders, either
mortgage-holders or purchasers of the land with
a view to the highest scale of profitable culti-
vation. On such estates the discipline is severe,
and the moral and social condition of the Negroes is truly pitiable. Away from the public
opinion of the North, which exercises more or
less of a modifying influence on slavery in the

H

Northern Slave States, they wear the yoke of bondage in its most galling form; there is no tongue to tell of hope, and no hand to guide to that land of blessed liberty which is only to be found far, far away on the banks of the St. Lawrence under the shadow of the British flag. On the other side, there are many naturally humane and kindly people, who give their slaves holidays, dances, and barbecues. Many a time, on the sunny shores of Georgia, amid groves of magnolias and palms, I have seen the slaves dancing to their own music ; and as their musical voices have sung " The Old Folks at Home" and " Oh carry me back to old Virginy," I have ceased to feel surprise at the way in which many travellers have been perverted into palliating the system. Besides these humane people, there are (paradoxical to some minds as it may appear) Christian slaveholders, who exercise a rigid moral supervision over their slaves, who deeply, yes, painfully, feel their own responsibilities, and who provide religious instruction and religious privileges for all who are connected with them, and who devote much of their own time to imparting *oral* instruction, the teaching of reading being prohibited by a

law which many Christian men seek to justify.
I believe, further, that hundreds of thousands
of slaves possess a *happiness* which is hardly
enjoyed by an equal number of any other race
in any other circumstances. With every want
supplied, without one care for the morrow, free
to love and to be loved, passionately fond of
music and dancing, of preaching, psalm-singing,
and praying, they enjoy that kind of happiness
which is described as " Pleased with a rattle,
tickled with a straw." They laugh with a
laughter which would prove infectious to the
most confirmed hypochondriac; they sing over
their work, and dance away the long summer
evenings; but to say that *slaves* are *happy* is to
bring the best argument which can be adduced
against the system. Cases of revolting cruelty
are occasionally brought to light, and even the
general and moderate use of the lash may justly
be condemned; but the charge of cruelty is one
of the weakest which can be brought against
the system, and only leads to mutual recrimi-
nations between England and America, by
which the interests of the slave are not at all
benefited.

I condemn slavery on higher, wider grounds,

and, abandoning altogether the discussion of its practice, adopt historic language which declares, in no faltering tones, that " all men are born free and equal, and have equal and inalienable rights to life, liberty, and the pursuit of happiness." And I take a "higher law" than the constitution which has so justly proclaimed the grand principles of human freedom, a law of undoubted authority and universal application, " As ye would that men should do to you, do ye even also to them;" and if those of my fellow Christians who contend for the justice of the decision—" *A coloured man has no rights which a white man is bound to respect*"—will conscientiously state that they will forego the rights of liberty, property, and indissoluble marriage, I will be content that the Negro shall suffer this triple deprivation, which constitutes the true essence and bitterness of slavery.

As my space will not allow me to take a general view of the Southern Churches, I will briefly regard them in connection with slavery, which is an integral part of all Southern organizations. Most of the wealthier and more highly-educated planters belong to the Episcopalian and Presbyterian Churches, and a warm attachment to the former is widely extended among them. The Episcopalian Church possesses some active bishops in the South, among whom I would particularise Bishop Elliott, of Georgia, and Bishop Meade, of Virginia. The former is a slaveholder to some extent, and is injudicious in his efforts to withdraw the Negroes from their favourite Baptist preachers and proselytise them to his own Church. The Southern Episcopalians are active, and there is much true and influential piety among them. There are large Presbyterian congregations in the cities, presided over by men of great pulpit power and earnest Christian zeal. The Methodist Episcopal Church has many thousands of adherents among the less-educated whites. The Negroes, wherever they are free to follow their own inclinations, attend the Baptist and Methodist Churches, and have many preachers of their own colour.

There is a visible influence of religion in the South, for which some would scarcely be prepared. In Richmond, Charleston, and the other Eastern cities, the Sabbath is well observed, and there is an external decorum of manners; in-

deed the older Southern States bear a not indis-
tinct resemblance to our agricultural counties.
The " good figs" are " very good," and, in spite
of slavery and even among the slaveholders,
there is a great deal of vital Christianity.   I
believe, further, that there are hundreds and
thousands of residents in the Southern States
who hate slavery more earnestly than many
Christian men in the North, are less of apolo-
gists for it, are less indifferent to its wants and
its woes, and are more in sympathy with that
spirit of liberty in the New Testament which has
consumed so much evil in the world and is destined finally to consume every vestige of slavery
and oppression.   There are hundreds of slaveholders who, possessing high ideas of Christian
responsibility, are untiring in their efforts to
promote the welfare of their slaves and carry
themselves towards them with a rigid conscien-
tiousness and Christian fidelity. Yet it is a noteworthy fact that the " Revival" has scarcely
penetrated into the Southern States, and that
the earnest and persevering prayers which have
ascended from Southern Christians have not
been answered by any marked outpouring of
the Holy Spirit.

In the newer States and in the old French section, inhabited by a mixed or unsettled population, the influence of religion diminishes, till in some parts of Texas and Arkansas it is scarcely perceptible. The Southern Churches are far less aggressive in their spirit than those of the North, and much spiritual destitution exists, for which the Southern Aid Society is providing a partial remedy. There are many districts in which the Gospel is only preached three or four times in the year, and where the sacramental ordinances of the Churches can scarcely be obtained. Some of the South-western cities are externally uninfluenced by religion, and New Orleans has attained an unenviable notoriety for its total contempt of law and order.

The manners of the Southerners are largely tinged with the chivalry of the middle ages, and seem consonant with the feudal customs which they have retained. The vice of intemperance attains a very great height. That family may be esteemed happy which has not one member at least a drunkard. Perhaps want of employment may be one cause of the prevalence of this vice among young men. Governor Wise said with a good deal of truth that the "young men of Virginia have nothing to do but lie on the graves of their grandfathers and drink brandy cocktails and gin sling." Men of all ages are to be seen in the country lounging about upon ungroomed horses, and in the cities slouching along the streets with cigars in their mouths, wearing their short cloaks and peaked hats with the true *hidalgo* air, or sipping spirituous mixtures, and talking local politics in the bar-rooms, or sitting in numbers outside the hotels in those extraordinary attitudes in which Americans indulge, apparently devoured with *ennui*. It is impossible to visit the South without observing the superabundance of what are popularly called "Loafers." Duelling is extremely common, and the most trivial disputes often have a bloody termination. The practice of carrying arms also frequently leads to fatal results; and throughout the Slave States law has attained what I would fain believe is its maximum point of weakness; and is occasionally bought and sold like any other commodity. The religious influence is not strong enough to exercise the powerful suasion which it has in the North. Apart from all the crime connected with slavery, I do not think favourably of the state of religion in the South. If the standards of doctrine are orthodox, Christian practice is too often inconsistent, the Churches are torpid, and their religious influence is not strong enough to counteract the admitted laxity of morals.

The pulpit exercises a most powerful influence in America; I doubt whether any practice could stand for many years before its denunciation, if pronounced unanimously. And here the great crime and plague-spot of the American Churches is seen. The great progress made by the slave power during the last thirty years is mainly to be attributed to them. Formerly the Southern planters whined over slavery as a weakness and as a disgrace; as an unavoidable evil which they would willingly be rid of. If the Churches had then taken a decided line, as they were bound to do, I believe that Slavery would be either now in process of abolition, or that the whole public sentiment of America would be arrayed against it. But under their influence, and with the sanction of the clergy, the South has come to regard Slavery as " a patriarchal institution, an ordinance of God, an equal advantage to the master and the slave, elevating both; as strength, wealth, and power; and as one of the main pillars and controlling influences of modern civilization." The Churches are bound up with the system; they are rich in human property; the bishops and clergy of the different denominations, the office-bearers, and the communicants, are slaveholders, and buy and sell their fellow-men, whom they profess to recognize as " temples of the Holy Ghost." I have heard Slavery extolled in Southern pulpits as the " only successful missionary institution which the world has ever seen." I have heard these words used in prayer in a Presbyterian church, by a minister of whose personal piety I entertain no doubt: " We thank thee, O Lord, that from a barbarous land, where idols are worshipped in blood and flame, thou hast brought a great multitude to our shores to sit at our feet and learn thy Gospel." The sacred marriage words, " Until death us do part," are perverted by Southern ministers, in the case of slaves, into " Until we are unavoidably separated;" and ministers of the highest position not only palliate, but approve, of this base outrage upon humanity! That Christian men and Christian ministers should unite to deprive men

of the power to read the Bible appears somewhat singular; but they know that the knowledge of reading would pull down the whole
structure of slavery and overturn its dark despotism. The practices of sophism and equivo-
cation to which Southern Christians resort, in
their attempts to sustain or palliate the evils of
slavery, affect the whole character, and their
minds, accustomed to a constant habit of tor-
tuous reasoning on one subject, become by no
means straightforward upon others; and their
love of a system which Christianity and reason
alike condemn produces in them a spirit of
malignity towards all who differ from them,
which is very unbecoming to a Christian profession. I believe that the Southern Churches
deserve all the accusations which the eloquent
tongue of Cheever has brought against them.
They are the mainstay and backbone of slavery;
they have led the South to review the subject,
and, by declaring Slavery to be an ordinance of
God, fostered by the New Testament, and a
noble missionary institution, they have turned
the tide of popular feeling, and have done more
to perpetuate the system than the whole mass
of Southern politicians. I abhor slavery, but

pity the slaveholder: he is the victim of an
hereditary curse, and inherits human property
fettered by the laws of his State, degraded in
bondage, helpless if free; and the Christianity
of his country, the ministers of the Churches
which profess to expound the will of God, have
aided, with all their might, to rivet the curse
upon him and his posterity for evermore.

The South now contains 4,000,000 of slaves,
who are all nominally Christians. Degraded
by the system under which they exist, they are
deficient in ambition, foresight, honesty, and
truth; and complete truthfulness, according to
our ideas of it, is not always seen among those
who are otherwise consistent. This moral degradation is not singular in the case of the
Negro. It is the inevitable consequence of all
prolonged tyrannies, whether political, ecclesiastical, or social. The case of the Israelites,
after their captivity under the Pharaohs, is an
instance. Where shall we find a baser, meaner
horde than that which Moses led up out of the
land of Egypt? True religion does much for
the slave; and thousands who wear the yoke of
earthly bondage are standing fast in the liberty
wherewith Christ has made them free. There

is something peculiarly touching and simple
about their faith and the way in which they
realize Christ as a living, present Saviour.
The character of "Uncle Tom" is, in this respect, no fiction. With a great deal of real
piety there is mingled, especially in the most
southerly States, a great deal of almost fanatical
enthusiasm, which is manifested by groans, ges-
tures, and outcries, which are by no means tra-
vestied in the accounts of camp-meetings in
" Dred." Whatever may be the effect produced
upon white people by the eccentricities of these
gatherings, they are seasons of great enjoyment
to the slaves. In the cities the Africans generally worship in plain churches. They prefer
coloured preachers, but recent local legislation
has greatly restricted their religious privileges
in some of the States. I am acquainted with a
flourishing black congregation which *bought* its
minister; but as slaves cannot hold property,
the transaction was carried on through a white
man, who holds the title-deeds, &c. Some of
these preachers are very forcible in their language, and not at all grotesque.

There is an African Baptist Church in Richmond which has more than 3,000 members,

who make a creditable Christian profession, and an account of a service in it may be interesting, as showing how Negroes worship God. The service was held on the last Sabbath of 1858, when Richmond was crowded with Negroes, who were to be sold or hired during the next week. The church was a plain, low building, in the form of the letter T, with deep galleries, and seated for 2,000 persons. It was closely packed on this occasion. The women sat in one half of the church, the men in the other. There were black men, with faces shining like well-polished boots, brown men, and yellow men; old men, whose grey wool contrasted strongly with their black skins, and young men dressed in the extreme of the fashion, all chewing tobacco. There were young girls, beautiful brunettes, with nothing but their slightly-crisped hair to indicate their African origin; huge, fat " mammies," with immense faces radiant with pleasure; and old smoke-dried crones, who sat swaying to and fro, their jaws moving ceaselessly. The young women were dressed in the gayest colours and the smallest bonnets, and wore, very inappropriately, the cast-off finery of their mistresses.

Before the minister arrived, the people were singing with mouths and eyes distended, and their feet beating time heavily; but probably their untaught praise discoursed sweeter music to Him who seeth not as man seeth than the harmonies of the cathedrals of all lands.

The minister first called upon an elder to pray. A eulogy upon this prayer may appear rather extravagant to those whose sole ideas of negro worship are derived from stories of the undisciplined exaggerations of "camp meetings," where the oddity of the ideas is only equalled by the grotesqueness of the language. This prayer, considered in all respects—appropriateness of language, manner, and matter—was well worthy to be preserved. Long before it was over tears were rolling down the cheeks of most of the white persons present; one wealthy slaveholder was crying outright, so great was the power of sublimity, simplicity, and pathos, even with the running accompaniment, on the part of the congregation, of moans, groans, and " Amens," and whispers, sufficiently audible, of " Oh, dear! Oh, grant it! Oh, Jesus!" The elder was a very dark mulatto, with woolly hair, flat nose, and thick lips, but with an intellectual forehead and a fine expression of countenance. His prayer commenced with a deep confession of sin; then followed a sublime expression of adoration of the goodness and wisdom of God, especially as evidenced in the scheme of redemption; next thanksgiving; and it might have shamed many a discontented heart to hear these enslaved mortals thanking God for their mercies. This was followed by petitions as comprehensive as those of the English Litany. (The hiring time was at the new year, five days afterwards, when about 3,500 Negroes changed masters, besides those who were sold.) In allusion to these changes, over which they had no control, he used these words: " Guide us in all our changes; take us not far from thine house; or, if we are removed from Zion's assemblies, may thy presence be better to us than an earthly temple. Oh, take us not where we shall be tempted above that we are able! Make us lowly, meek, and consistent, so like Christ that we may win others to love Him. We have met through one year as brethren; may we all meet where time is neither measured by years, nor marked by changes, in the holier Jerusalem above, where sin is done with, where partings are unknown, and where God himself shall wipe all tears from our eyes!"

The earnestness and scriptural nature of the sentiments would not have surprised those who are conversant with negro piety, but the language and manner were very remarkable. The elder spoke the very best English with distinct articulation and pure pronunciation. I never observed that another word could have been substituted with advantage for any that he used; his voice was rich and well modulated; his manner was deeply reverential; and, apart from the beauty of his ideas and sentiments, his language and style would have pleased the ear and taste of the most educated audience. The minister preached an excellent sermon, dwelling on practice rather than on doctrine, which was followed by two admirable prayers. The crowd began to disperse after this, but was detained by an outburst of loud but harmonious singing, which was continued until the shades of evening warned all to their homes.

And here were men bound to us, not only by a common humanity, but by the stronger ties of a common Christianity, children of the same God, co-heirs of the same immortality, many of

I

whom are doubtless to inherit the Paradise to
come; but " chattels," of whom the highest
legal authority in the land has declared that
" they possess no rights which a white man is
bound to respect."* They are born to a heritage
of 'bondage; legislation has sought to quench
within their breasts every emotion of love and
hope; they possess no indissoluble marriage, no
liberty, no country, and no home. Their virtues
win no admiration, and their wrongs no sympathy; they have no holier rights than the
beasts of the field; yet this is the system which
Southern Christians hug and palliate, and before which the Churches lick the dust. Before
another Sabbath many of the worshippers in
this church were sold in the streets and auction-
rooms of Richmond; wives separated from hus-
bands, fathers from children, sent down, under
the selfish care of mercenary traders, to toil
without reward among the dreary rice swamps
of the Carolinas, or the lonely sugar plantations
of Alabama and Mississippi, where the cry of
the bondsman reaches no ear and pierces no

---

* *Vide* decision of the Supreme Court of the United
States in the celebrated " Dred Scott" case.

heart but that of Him who has commanded to
" let the oppressed go free, and break every
yoke."

Shortly after this period a slave stood on the
auction block, in the town of L ——, surrounded
by traders and others. After displaying the
athletic form of the " chattel" the auctioneer
eulogised him thus: " Him's a nigger as good
as you could see, rising twenty-eight, sound as
an oak, *honest, industrious, sober;* haint the mark
of a lash upon him." The first bid was a thousand dollars. " You could trust him with your
wife and your children, your keys and your
money."—1,100, 1,200 dollars. " He was con-
verted four years ago, he's as good as a preacher
among yer cattle."—1,250, 1,300, 1,400 dollars.
" He's got the Holy Spirit; he can pray, and
sing, and preach; he keeps all the Commandments; he can preach like the Bishop himself."
And after a spirited competition the Christian
slave, the elder of a Southern Church, was
" knocked down" for 1,850 dollars.

The strength, youth, and capabilities of the
slave sold for 1,200 dollars; his Christianity, the
life of the Spirit of God within him, for 650
dollars more! Truly there are few countries

where Christianity is prized so highly! The great point to which I would direct attention is this, that the orthodox Churches of the South are the great bulwarks of slavery. They commit the glaring inconsistency of sending Missionaries to teach the Africans in Africa to read, while they sustain the prohibition of the same privilege to the Africans in America. It is a grievous thing that the latest born of mighty nations, the best taught, the richest in the heritage of all great things that martyrs, and confessors, and dying patriots have bequeathed to the world, is the most recreant of all Christian nations to the law of love, the most haughty to the weak, the most despotic to the helpless. If there is one other thing more melancholy and shameful it is to see Churches established for no other end than the propagation of Gospel moralities refusing to bear a testimony in favour of 4,000,000 men infested with every immorality which oppression can create, weighed down with every evil which the Gospel was intended to alleviate, and destroyed by every malignant mischief from which the Gospel was meant to be a salvation. The Christianity of the South, vitiated by sophistries and equivocations, never rises above a certain level, for religious progress is incompatible with a compromise with evil, and he who holds in his terrible hand the scales of "even-handed justice" will not stay the consequences of a wilful sophism, even for the best of men. Before the eye of the love of God, and under the genial glow of an enlightened Christianity, the distinctions of race and colour vanish. There is but one Father Universal; there is but one Family; there is but one Brotherhood; and throughout all the races and infinite numbers of men there is not a stranger, an alien, a foreigner! We are all brethren and members one of another!

CHAPTER VIII.— *The Aspects of the West.*

HE West considered as to the future is the most interesting portion of America. It is the fitting theatre where one of the greatest problems of human destiny is being worked out; a theatre on which are congregated the representatives of the leading races and of all the leading moral, social, and religious tendencies out of which the end is to be elaborated. The problem is vast, and the scene of its evolution is commensurate with its greatness. It needs but a journey from the Atlantic to St. Louis to be impressed with the boundless magnificence of the material basis of the West. One day carries us, as on the wings of the wind, through the cities, the villages, and the wheatfields of New York; the next we traverse the waves of one of the noblest of inland seas; the third trans-

ports us through the deep recesses of majestic
forests; the fourth we are swept along over
prairies so vast as to bewilder the imagination
as it vainly attempts to recal them; and even
then we have not spanned half the continent on
those rims of steel, but have only reached the
great central artery of the West, the mighty
Mississippi, with its twenty thousand miles of
navigable tributaries, and its rich valley, fruitful enough to sustain a population as large as
that of Europe; and all along this course are
towns and cities, the creation of yesterday,
hardly less wonderful than the country in which
they are planted, instinct with life, with the
appliances of civilization, for which Europe and
Asia have been ransacked, brought to the very
doors; and all this wealth of lake, prairie, and
forest, is but the material substratum of Western civilization. More tongues are spoken
within the western borders than in the Roman
Empire in its palmiest days. More races are
there congregated than ever before met under
an equal government, making the prairies re-
sound and the forests tingle with their appeals
for the equal rights of man. There meet the
extremes of black and white: the Asiatics, al-

ready swarming on the Pacific coast; the native
Indians, disdaining subjugation, for ever following the setting sun; the Caucasian, in its
three leading varieties of German, Celt, and
Anglo-Saxon; and in the midst of all these the
tone is given and the march is led by that one
of them which has never yet faltered in its onward course, which can migrate to all climes,
and which is possessed of such tenacity and
versatility that it is everywhere successful. In
the West the great tendencies of the times are
developing themselves with a rapidity elsewhere
unknown, and are able to press forward to their
ends as nowhere else, being assisted by the
character of the government and by the separation between Church and State. There meet
the men of all civilized kindreds and tongues,
and they are mingling together and growing up
a united race, amidst institutions free as the air
of heaven.

The population of the West is a very mixed
one. It is composed of native-born Americans,
many of them from the New England States,
English, Irish, Scotch, Scandinavians, Germans,
French, Portuguese, and Italians. The characteristics of the various nations, though modified

by a uniform political system, are very marked. The Englishman brings with him an athletic body and an uncultivated mind, too often intemperate habits, and a confirmed unconcern about his religious welfare; the Irishman brings with him his Popery and his priests, his recklessness, his genial qualities, and his love of kindred; the Scotchman his solid education, his exclusive feelings of nationality, and his steadfastness of purpose; the German his skilled industry, his frugal habits, his social and religious theories, and often his infidelity; the Frenchman his levity and loose morality; the Italian his deep hatred of the tyranny from which he has escaped. All these have aspirations after something better than they have known; a something which is frequently eluding their grasp, teaching them that there is no Eden on this side Paradise; that no Golden Age exists even under the glittering star of " popular sovereignty," and that vice and crime have their penalties in America as well as in Europe.

The last thing which emigrants think of is a provision for religious worship. The idle and the visionary, who are disappointed with the El Dorado of their dreams, those who are ex-

patriated for their crimes, penniless demagogues
whose sole capital consists in a grievance, un-
principled adventurers, and the renegade outpourings of all Europe and all America, mingle
in a conglomerate mass with the virtuous, the
respectable, and the industrious. With such
discordant materials, it is not a matter of surprise that some of the worst features of the Old
World are reproduced in the New, that law
should lose something of its force, that fanatics
and sectaries should gain numerous adherents,
that every *ism* should be rampant, and that evil
should be occasionally, though generally tem-
porarily, triumphant.   The emissaries of evil
have been unremitting in their attempts to sub-
jugate the West.   Romish priests, infidel pro-
pagandists, professed reformers of society on
socialist principles, and Mormon agents, have
formed a phalanx on the side of the " god of this
world."   On the side of good, in the early stages
of Western progress, the agencies appear feeble ;
they consist in great measure of emigrants from
the New England States, who carry with them
the leaven of religion and morality, the Sabbath, the meeting-house, and the school; and
noble men, imbued with the true missionary

spirit, who brave the discomforts of border life
and the chills and fever of newly-cleared soils
for the sake of Him whose high commission
they bear. If any human works were worthy
of a record on high, it would be such deeds of
missionary devotion; and those who perform
them and succumb to the diseases of the climate
may well be reckoned among "the noble army
of martyrs." Although in many districts there
is much religious destitution, the advantage has
decidedly been won by true Christianity, and
the West evidences a powerful religious influence. This desirable and hardly to be expected
result has been brought about partly by the
increased emigration of respectable persons
from the Eastern States, who have leavened
the mass of European emigration, and who,
regarding provision for religious worship as a
necessity, have organized Churches and Sabbath-
schools; partly by those two Catholic and powerful agencies, the American Tract Society and
the American Sunday School Union; partly by
the Eastern Churches, who see in the whitening
harvests of the West a call to more energetic
Evangelical effort, by means of Home Missionary Societies; partly by that law of pro-

gress which observation compels us to recognize; and, beyond all these, by that gracious Spirit whose invisible agency, moving like the wind, has breathed a revival influence over the mighty West.

In Ohio, Michigan, Indiana, and Illinois, society has a more settled aspect, and the Churches possess organizations as perfect as those of New York. The Church edifices of Chicago, Cincinnati, Detroit, Cleveland, &c. are built and fitted with taste and elegance. One church at Chicago, in the florid Gothic style, may safely compete with All Saints, Margaret-street. The comfort of the interiors of these churches, as of churches generally in America, certainly disposes persons to devotion and attention. The Western ministers are often of great pulpit power, and in the settled districts the church-accommodation bears a due proportion to the wants of the people.

The State of Ohio, although not more than forty years old, is nearly as settled as the State of New York. It may be said of it, and of many parts of Indiana, Illinois, and Michigan, that the population differs from that of the Eastern States principally in being less aris-

tocratic, less educated, and more locomotive.
Religion in Ohio is very influential, and two
names connected with it are widely known and
much respected in England, Bishop McIlvaine
and the Rev. C. Finney. The first combines
great learning with Apostolic power and missionary zeal; the last is very eminent in the
pulpit, and for his lectures on revivals, and has
established Oberlin College, a somewhat celebrated educational institution. Indiana exhibits
less of the religious influence, but her Sabbath
laws are very strict and her Sabbath-school
system very efficient. The southern part of
Michigan differs little from Ohio. Even in the
villages of recent erection provision has been
made for religious worship. I spent some time
in a forest settlement, the oldest house in which
was fifteen years old, and, with a population of
500 souls, it had five Churches under the super-
intendence of ministers of Evangelical sentiments. Michigan owes much to the unwearied
labours of Dr. Duffield and Mr. Paterson, of
the Presbyterian Church, and to the energy of
Bishop McCoskray, although his sentiments
are not Evangelical. The northern peninsula
of Michigan, between Mackinaw Straits and

Lake Superior, has been settled very much by Welsh and Cornish miners. Efforts are made for their good; but certainly this section of the country has more appearance of irreligion than any which I visited. In eastern Illinois and southern Wisconsin, although the population *is* a very mixed one, the religious influence is still strong, sufficiently so to act as a powerful check upon the heterogeneous mass. In the large cities, Chicago, Milwaukee, &c. the German element is very powerful, amounting to a fourth, frequently to a third, of the population. The Germans do not always observe the Sabbath as a day of physical rest; and in the German quarter of these towns many of the stores are habitually open. Still, if a general view of these cities be taken, the observance of the Sabbath is a most impressive feature. The stores are generally closed, travelling ceases, few vehicles are to be seen in the streets, the Sabbath-schools and churches are thronged, and an air of decorum pervades all things. This is most remarkable in the huge city of Chicago, that prodigy of the Western Continent, which, during the six days of the week, seems hardly to know an interval of repose, business fre-

quently being carried on by night as well as by
day. On the Sabbath the stillness is very observable; the hush has something almost portentous about it, and is broken principally by
the trampling of thousands of feet to and from
service. In nearly a direct line from Chicago
are Galena, on Fever River, and Dubuque, on
the Mississippi, which may be taken as fair
specimens of mushroom progressive Western
towns, characterized by continual bustle. Galena is perfectly reposeful on the Sabbath, and
the stores are all closed. At Dubuque, although the boats to and from St. Louis create
some bustle at the "levee," most of the people
who are seen in the streets are going to and
from worship, and the contrast between Saturday and Sunday is as great as can be imagined.
On the Ohio, the Missouri, and the Mississippi
there are numerous small settlements, hardly
distinguishable from the forest, which have no
resident ministers, and where the river traffic,
which knows no cessation, produces Sabbath
desecration. The city of St. Paul, containing
16,000 inhabitants, is situated on the Mississippi, 2,200 miles from the Gulf of Mexico;
and here, where we should least expect it, after

winding for days through rock and dense forest
along the devious mazes of this mighty stream,
we find that flourishing religious organizations
have preceded many of the accessories of civilization, and that there are fourteen Churches
with respectable edifices presided over by efficient ministers. The observance of the Sabbath
and the influence of religion in this city of the
wilderness have been commented upon by many
travellers. This repose on the Sabbath is often
the result of necessity rather than choice.
Many men who are in the West on business
would prefer to travel on the Sabbath if they
could, but few " through " trains run on Sunday.
Some railroads only run one train during the
day, and on others there is no travelling at all.
The strict Sabbath laws of the Western States
are the most powerful testimony to the physical
value of the Sabbath. They are the expression
of the will of the sovereign people, and of the
conviction of the busiest and most restless population on earth, that one day of rest in seven is
absolutely necessary for the physical, moral, and
intellectual well-being of man.

Beyond these States, whose religious aspects
I have imperfectly sketched, lies that vast " Far

West," whose location it is difficult to define, for the frontier of civilization is ever moving onwards. The axes of its hardy pioneers are heard among the forests which surround the sources of the Missouri and the La Platte; the vast tide of population is breaking upon the shores of the Pacific, and a few years will probably witness the transit of railroad trains through the defiles of the Rocky Mountains. The Far West is where new communities are battling with the forest trees for space on which to sow their grain; where the Red Indian pursues the buffalo over interminable prairies; where the peaks of the Rocky Mountains gleam purple in the setting sun—the grim barriers of Western progress. The Far West, at whose religious aspects I propose to glance, is composed of Western Illinois, Northern Wisconsin, Western Iowa, Kansas, Nebraska, Minnesota, and Western Missouri. In these States few, if any, of the adult inhabitants are natives of the States in which they are now located, and they have received whatever of education they possess, and have formed their habits both for good and evil, before they arrive in the Far West.

All intelligent readers are familiar with the

K

" Border Ruffianism " of Missouri; with Kansas, surrendered to be the battle-ground of conflicting parties, baptized at first in blood and flame, and subsiding into a chronic state of insecurity; with tales of Indian warfare on the frontiers of civilization; with the lawlessness of the Mississippi river, and the recklessness of human life displayed on the numerous steamers which traverse its mighty waters; it is not necessary to enlarge on such things as these, or upon the anarchy which, in the opinion of some persons, threatens to pervade the Western States. The good is more surprising than the evil; a rude code of honour is observed everywhere, and a marked deference to and respect for females, worthy of the most polite circles, is universal even in the wildest districts.   In the Far West there is a vast scattered population dwelling on the prairies and in the forests, and about one-half of this population is not brought under the influence of any Gospel means regularly dispensed. But among these people, many of whom, if left to themselves, would subside into a state almost worse than heathenism, the labours of the Home Missionary, and Tract Society, and Sunday-school Union, have been

signally blessed.   The first of these is continually sending missionaries into destitute districts,
and organizing Churches; the second is engaged
in preparing the soil by annually disseminating
millions of useful publications.   In the three
States of Illinois, Iowa, and Missouri, this Society has employed from thirty to sixty col-
porteurs per annum, who, during the past year,
have visited nearly 60,000 families; and abundant proof has been granted that their humble
labours have not been in vain.   The Sunday-
school Union is yet more efficient; during the
past five years it has organized above 12,000
schools, containing 78,000 teachers and 540,000
scholars.   In the West the Sabbath-school is
frequently, as in the Western Islands of Scotland, the earliest religious organization.   Assisted
by the Central Union a few godly people establish a Sabbath-school in a prairie or forest
settlement, which awakens a religious interest in
the young; the parents are soon aroused, prayer-
meetings are established, expositions of Scripture are given, a rude church is erected, and a
minister is called to look after " the sheep in
the wilderness."   His residence is frequently
only a log hut, and the small stipends which

these settlements can afford to offer are supplemented of necessity by " surprise parties," and " donation meetings." The Society for promoting Collegiate Education in the West, which now aids sixteen infant colleges, is doing much to train up an Evangelical ministry for these new districts ; for there, as elsewhere, the same tale may be told of a plenteous harvest and few labourers. No earthly ambitions and no views of earthly aggrandisement enter the minds of those ministers who go out to the Far West. The hardships are great and the emoluments small, the necessaries of life are often difficult to obtain ; a portion of the country is " locked in regions of thick-ribbed ice" for five months of the year; the refinements of educated society are unknown ; lawlessness, coarseness of manners, and moral degradation, are common, and occasionally at first the message and the messenger are alike contemned. But it is among the heterogeneous population which I have elsewhere described that the Gospel is achieving some of its mightiest triumphs ; and within the past year ministers who have laboured long in hope upon the distant prairies have been called to gather in a more abundant harvest

than their prolific soil has ever yielded. The
wilderness and the solitary place have been glad
for them, and the desert has rejoiced and blos-
somed as the rose. The toils and hardships of
ministerial life are shared by those who have
been elected by the Churches to hold the chief
offices, and it may interest readers accustomed
only to English luxury to know how a missionary bishop lives in the Far West.

We had left railroads far behind, and after
traversing for seven days the noble inland seas
of Superior, Huron, and Michigan, we had
toiled along for some time in wagons drawn by
mules. Even the rude roads of the West had
disappeared, and we pursued a track made by
the pioneers of civilization. The forest was
sometimes entirely unbroken, its giant trees
towering high above and producing a dusky
twilight below; then a partial clearing with the
log cabin of the first settler, with the corn
growing among the charred and blackened
stumps of trees. Then there would be a tract
of land covered with huge trees, with leafless
stems, having been "girdled" the preceding
year as the first step towards their removal.
Again there would be undulating plains or

" oak openings," country covered with trees
in clumps and without underwood, presenting
the appearance of a natural park. The country
selected for the " Episcopal Palace" was forest
land. The " Palace" stood on a clearing of a
few acres in the depths of a great forest, and
presented the appearance of a small cottage with
three windows and a door. It was the first
building erected by a settler, and very rude in
its appearance, with everything to remind us
that we were fifteen hundred miles from the
Atlantic seaboard, with the primæval trees of
the West rustling around us. The almost
torrid heat of the day was over, the evening
breeze was sighing through the forest, the fireflies had already lit their lamps in the shade,
and the rich sunset light was quivering through
the foliage and dancing upon the soil. The
Bishop had preached twice during the day at
rude Churches twelve miles distant from each
other, and after his days' work was sitting outside his cabin mending a chair. The house
contained neither parlour nor library; books
and papers were packed away in boxes; hardships and difficulties were on every side. In
the long winters there is rarely any commu-

nication with the exterior world; six weeks sometimes elapse without any mail. For about eight months of the year this bishop is engaged in travelling over the section of country which he regards as his diocese, " in perils by land and by water ;" now under a burning sun crossing a prairie two hundred miles in length, with few signs of habitation; now in districts where roads there are none, following the deepworn Indian trail through otherwise trackless forests; now in the terrible winter travelling on snow-shoes; and now on some of the swelling streams of the West trusting himself to a frail canoe. Some idea may be formed from this of the hardships which ministers with smaller stipends are forced to undergo in the West, but which are cheerfully and trustfully borne for their great Master's sake.

Yet, perhaps, this itinerating life, with all its hardships, is more agreeable than some other fields of Western labour. While in the desolate rockbound regions bordering upon Lake Superior, I saw a pastor of high education and cultivated tastes who had been labouring for two years in a wild district which is generally shut out from communication with the civilized world for seven months of the year. He is surrounded by the roughest description of emigrants. He has worked zealously but with little success. He has two log-rooms at a distance of ten miles from each other, where he holds services, and this distance is often traversed for five months of the year on snow-shoes. His log hut contains one room with a curtain partition, and there is not a creature in the neighbourhood with whom he can hold congenial converse. It is a missionary work with more than missionary hardships; but by such means is the West evangelized. This pastor is the *one civilizing influence* of the district, working slowly but surely. His mission is the *one hope* for the social and religious advancement of that locality, and is breaking the fallow ground and sowing the seed where a few years will witness a scattered population expanding into a great people.

We have now glanced at the New England States with their steady habits, and their hereditary inheritance of an orthodox faith, and at the South with its strange contrasts and hereditary curse. In the West and Far West we have a country differing widely from both—a land without tradition, history, or inheritance—a nation of yesterday, whose growth and progress form one of the most remarkable phenomena of modern history. Upon the boundless plains of the Western States are gathered all nations, kindreds, and tongues, freed from many of the restraints which guard the faith and restrain the excesses of older communities. To swell the concourse, thousands and tens of thousands are annually pouring in a perennial stream of emigration from Europe and the older States, led by the star of empire which still glitters in the West, and seems to pause only upon the Rocky Mountains to point out the barrier of Western civilization. In a short space of time each emigrant becomes a citizen of the second Protestant empire in the world; an empire which has known no retrogression—whose frontier is ever advancing, and whose future promises to be more wondrous than its past. It is well indeed that in a mere political point of view America is alive to the importance and exigencies of a population which will soon hold in its hands the balance of power, and dictate measures at Washington. It is well that even worldly men recognize religion, as the only coercive power which can be brought to bear on these masses, the only influence which can be successfully exercised in favour of law and order. In this respect the Evangelization of the West assumes a universal importance.

With all the evils attendant upon unsettled communities, heterogeneous population, and weak government, the influence of religion in the Western States is very evident and very powerful, and is a cause of thankfulness for the present as well as of hope for the future. The power of the Gospel is nowhere more apparent. It finds diverse, and occasionally antagonistic, races, and, assisted by a common government and a common education, it blends and harmonises them by the influence of a common Christianity. It finds arranged against it the mighty influences of Infidelity and Popery, and triumphs over the one, and promises in a few generations to destroy the power of the other; it finds the elements of lawlessness existing, and by its own influence it produces a respect for law and order; it finds men engrossed with the world's whirl of business, rising early, and late taking rest; and it induces them, by its moral power, exercised on their consciences, to give up one day in seven to God. The Church, the Sabbath-school, and the common school, are now accompanying the wave of population as it rolls Westward, leavening the mighty mass, and enabling the Christian to see, in the triumphant march of the dominant Anglo-Saxon race across the American Continent, one grand part of the Divine scheme for the spread of that Gospel which shall overthrow all opposition and survive all changes, and achieve its mightiest triumphs in the last days of our world's history.

CHAPTER IX.—*Characteristics of American Preaching.*

REACHING is one of the few sub- jects which may be judged without continual reference to the three great sections of the Union. It is a subject likewise of the highest importance, for preaching is the first duty of an organized ministry, the recognized instrument of the world's regeneration, the mould in which the moral sentiment of a nation is cast, the grand fulfilment of our Lord's latest, and most com- prehensive command with reference to the pro- mulgation of his everlasting Gospel. Perhaps in no country is the character of preaching of more importance than in America, where the masses of the people attend church, and where thousands and tens of thousands have little lei- sure for thought and less for reading, and over whose minds the teaching of the pulpit must necessarily exercise a most powerful influence. The number of attendants on public worship is unusually large in proportion to the population, judging by the English standard, and the number of men and young men at church cannot fail to strike a stranger's attention. In fact, attendance at church is considered a necessary sign of respectability; and whether men go to church to gain a gloss to their character, to satisfy their consciences, to stimulate their intellectual powers, to repose from the ceaseless ring of dollars and the whirl of speculation, or to spend an hour free from the din of crowded hotels, certain it is that in the Northern States, and in a lesser degree in the South and West, the mass of the educated population is to be seen at church, and habitual neglect in respectable circles is regarded rather as a sign of "rowdyism." Again, the pulpit in America is the only permanent depository of truth. All else is progressive, changeable, variable, destitute of fixed boundaries and landmarks. Neither is there any *universal* public standard of morals by which actions are judged and condemned. A species of moral obliquity pervades a class of the community which incapacitates the individuals composing it from discerning between truth and falsehood, except as either tends to their personal aggrandisement. Thus, from want of any other authority, the pulpit has naturally become not only the depository of truth, but the tribunal of appeal on all questions of moral right, and the purity of its ethics is of scarcely less importance than the soundness of its doctrine. Taking these circumstances, and others which I have not space to dwell upon, into consideration, I have no hesitation in attributing to the American pulpit an influence greater than is possessed by any other pulpit in the world.

During my residence in America I have heard sermons from about 130 ministers, and have read the printed discourses of about half as many more. I have heard sermons in the polished Atlantic cities, in the churches of the aristocracy of the South, in churches where slaves were ministers and auditors, in churches in infant settlements, and in those " forest sanctuaries " of which the roof is the dome of heaven. I have heard sermons by ministers of all the orthodox denominations, and yet, with opportunities for forming a judgment which have

fallen to the lot of few, I feel that it is a bold
step to hazard an opinion. Of course the varieties in style, manner, and substance must be
very numerous among such a large body of
preachers, many of whom have received the
very highest education, while quite a number of
the Baptist and Methodist preachers have had
but very few advantages. In the Episcopalian,
Congregational, and Presbyterian Churches,
with the various branches of the latter, it is usual
for ministers to go through a very severe course
of study. This course comprises the ordinary
college education, which is equal, and in some
respects superior, to that given in our Universi-
ties, and extends over a period of four years,
and a three years' course in a Theological Seminary, with a reference to the ministry during
the whole period of study. These Theological
Seminaries, of which there are thirty-seven, are
well worthy of our attention. The Princeton
course (from which few of the other seminaries
greatly vary) comprises for the first year, He-
brew, the exegesis of the original language of
the New Testament, sacred geography, sacred
chronology, Jewish antiquities, and the connection of sacred and profane history; for the

second year, Biblical criticism, Church history, and didactic theology; for the third year, polemic theology, Church government, pastoral theology, and the composition and delivery of sermons. The students read essays of their own composition once in four weeks, and deliver short addresses before the professors and their fellow-students once a month. One evening in each week is devoted to the discussion of important theological questions. Every Sabbath afternoon the students assemble for a " conference " on some subject in casuistical divinity, the professors presiding and closing the discussion with their remarks, and the services commencing and closing with singing and prayer. Such questions as the following, together with a hundred others, are discussed:— " What constitutes a call to the ministry, and the evidences of it? What is proper preparation for the Lord's Supper? What is repentance? What is faith? What is a true preparation for death?" Few men do more than the professors in these seminaries for the cause of Christ. Many of them, in addition to their stated duties, preach much in vacant churches, and before ecclesiastical assemblies and benevo-

lent and literary societies. Many employ their
little leisure in instructing the people through
the press. Among them are to be found, both
as respects talent and piety, many of the first
ministers of the Churches to which they respec-
tively belong, and all have given evidence of
their piety by lives of devotion and faithfulness.
Their great object is to train up a pious as well
as a learned ministry. Each one of them opens
the meeting of his class with earnest prayer, in
which he is joined by his pupils.

This thorough training, preceded by a college
education, has fitted about 10,000 of the living
ministers of the United States for their labours,
and in it, I think, we must recognize one of
the main foundations of their efficiency. They
come forth skilled in the use of every weapon
calculated to parry the assaults and destroy the
power of all the errors with which they may
hereafter meet.

Most of the Episcopalian and Congregational,
with a majority of the Presbyterian, and some
of the Baptist and Methodist ministers, read
their sermons; and those who do not, carefully
study the subjects of them, and use notes of the
principal divisions. Those of the clergy who

have passed through a regular classical and
theological course of education generally are *less*
animated in their delivery than the celebrated
preachers of Great Britain and Ireland. In
the Baptist, Methodist, and Cumberland Presbyterian denominations, where many of the
ministers have not had a classical education,
and do not read their sermons, the energy and
fervour of the manner are often very remarkable. Among the less-educated itinerant preachers a great deal of homely energetic eloquence
is to be met with, which is more likely to be-
nefit many of the audiences which they are
called upon to address than the more correct
and graceful diction of more learned men.

The ministry in the various Churches em-
braces, I think, greater intellectual power and
ability than any other profession, and truly it
is creditable to the nation to consecrate so many
men of the highest intellect and attainments to
the service of God. The intellectual character
of the preaching in some of the city churches
is very marked; and I certainly have listened
to sermons which were rather remarkable as
being finished literary efforts than for any more
useful quality ; and there is a disposition in

America, as elsewhere, to deify these intellectual giants of the pulpit.

Happily, however, in the orthodox Churches
throughout the United States the influence of
the pulpit is exerted almost exclusively for good.
The great sectional and denominational differences exercise scarcely any influence on the
preaching of the Gospel.   The same truths,
spoken in polished language to polished auditors
in Boston and Philadelphia, are heard in the
swamps of the Carolinas and in the sugar plantations of the Gulf States, and come echoing
back in more homely tones from the coasts of
the distant Pacific, the forest-bounded log-set-
tlements on the Western rivers, and the rockbound shores of Lake Superior.   In short,
wherever the English language is spoken (with
the solitary exception of the Mormon territory),
from the Canadian frontier to the Mexican
Gulf, and from the shores of the Atlantic to
those of the peaceful sea, the inhabitants of all
the cities and villages have the opportunity of
hearing the glad tidings of salvation.   The
Churches of America are all agreed on the great
essentials of doctrine, and in holding before the
eyes of sinners " Jesus Christ and him cruci-

fied," and to this we may trace their remarkable influence and efficiency. The American pulpit, as if fully aware of its unusual responsibilities, utters no wavering or uncertain sound, but, as a whole, in North, South, and West, except in the churches of some clergy who impose ceremonial teaching upon their people, the preaching is entirely Evangelical; and within the limits of the Churches we do not find those perilous extremes of Tractarian, Broad Church, Ultra-Calvinist, and Antinomian, which corrupt and deform our English denominations. Each Church possesses the supreme ecclesiastical authority, and if the conventions and synods are occasionally too rigorous in its exercise, if the Broad Churchman be driven to Unitarianism or Universalism, the Tractarian to the Romish Church, and the hyper-Calvinist and Antinomian to found sects for themselves, the error is excised from the Churches, instead of remaining, as too often with us, a festering sore.

There are churches in America where Gothic arches and delicate Saracenic tracery rejoice and distract the eye of the worshipper, where the " dim religious light" streams through windows of rich stained glass, and voices of seraphic sweetness pour forth strains of exquisite harmony from behind carved oaken screens, and light and music and architectural beauty combine to steep the senses in an atmosphere of spurious devotion. Such edifices hardly seem places for the simple setting forth of Him who " had no form or comeliness;" yet even from their pulpits denunciations of sin are fulminated, and the Cross of Christ is lifted up as the only hope of pardon and of peace. And there are simpler places of worship, with whitewashed walls and plain deal pews, where the poor are found, and where the slaves learn of a liberty wherewith Christ makes His people free. They are scattered over the South and over the villages of the West, but echo to the same Gospel. And there are congregations which meet to worship in temples which are not made with hands, with the sky for the roof and the earth for the floor, and with a blackened stump, or the end of a rude wagon, for a pulpit; but the same Gospel is preached to them by the zealous home missionary and " stump preacher "— Christ crucified, the sinner's only hope.

The *aimless* style of preaching so prevalent here is rarely to be met with in America.

The *ceremonial* preaching which exists in some congregations is continually swept away by the hurricanes of religious awakening which from time to time sweep over the land. America presents a spectacle foreign to our practice if not to our notions of bold Evangelization. The revived and ardent Christianity of that country of singular discrepancies has deposed or transformed the perfunctory sermonizer, and the good old-fashioned shepherd reposing quietly in the midst of his flock. Pastors who stood in the way of an aggressive style of preaching have long ere this found the current of public opinion too strong for them. The lifeless preaching and the moral essays which disfigure so many of our English pulpits are not tolerated in America. The people are too energetic to pardon dreary platitudes or vague and glittering generalities; they demand and they have something life-like—something which brings them into contact with the world to come—something which removes them from their sordid six-day cares into an atmosphere of holiness and perchance of hope. The highly-educated congregations of the Atlantic cities have learned to prize the " tongue of fire," and the crowded

pews and thronged aisles of the churches where
the Gospel is preached in its simplicity attest
the truth of the opinion of Professor Huntingdon
of (the Unitarian) Harvard College, that " nothing but the Gospel of the Son of God will
satisfy that craving thirst which exists in every
human nature, or awake an echo in any human
heart."

The name of Jonathan Edwards is associated
in many minds with New England. His system
of theology still affords a theme for discussion
to the divines of Europe and America; but
though scarcely greater as a theologian than as
a metaphysician, his preaching possessed all the
apostolic attributes and shook America as
Whitefield's once shook England. Many of his
successors were men of great mental endowments, but destitute of deep spirituality, and
for a period in the history of the New England
Churches the fiery eloquence of Edwards was
replaced by a style of preaching which it was
supposed would suit the tastes of the analytical
New England mind. Abstruse erudition, system, calmness, profundity of reflection, subtle
reasoning, everything which, according to the
ordinary rules of human thought, would give

religion a mastery over the intellects of mankind was pressed into the service of the pulpit. Perhaps no Church ever possessed greater elements of pulpit power; but the "tongue of fire" was wanting, errors crept in, and whole congregations fell into the Arian heresy. Now throughout the orthodox Churches of New England a simple Evangelical style of preaching prevails. Never has it been my lot to hear preaching more conformable to the simplicity and depth of Peter and Paul than in the cities and villages of that section of the country. The baptism of fire seems to have descended upon the preachers, and, mighty in that peculiar attribute, they are bending before them a nation of minds as strong and indomitable as ever bowed before the majesty of religious truth. I have seen, and that not in a time of "revival," men, old and young, silently weeping under the power of a discourse which, probing the recesses of their hearts, set their sins before them, and besought them in Christ's stead to be reconciled to God, and this, too, in the most polished city in America. This modern New England preaching is not fruitful alone in "conversions," numerous as these are, but it has raised a standard of pure morality, it has arrested the tide of error, and has won back whole congregations to orthodoxy; it has grappled with the sin of intemperance, and has rendered wine upon the table as unfashionable as disreputable, making total abstinence in some Churches a condition of Church membership. It studiously abstains from politics; but by raising a consistent voice against Slavery it has moved the mind of New England as that of one man against this monstrous iniquity. Its vast power is owing to the zeal, consistency, and piety of the clergy, their uncompromising faithfulness, and their simple preaching of the Gospel.

Passing over the West, where the preaching has many of the same admirable characteristics, I turn to the Far West, that seething, shoreless ocean, composed of people of all nations, creeds, and customs. Here the pulpit is the only moral influence, and if law and order have any power, to it they are indebted for it. Here the pulpit, throwing aside the conventional phraseology which is suitable only for educated ears, adopts itself to the tastes and comprehensions of the rude emigrants, and gains a power over them. On logs by the Missouri, the Upper Mississippi,

or the St. Louis, such congregations assemble
as could not be found in any other country.
They are composed almost entirely of men—
rude emigrants, hunters, trappers, pioneers, adventurers of every description, the *débris*, the
outpourings of society—men who are the foam
of civilization, and move ever as its advanced
guard; whose pride is in throwing off restraints,
whose lips pour forth profanity, and who in
their actions own no law.   Yet when the
preacher arrives a hush steals over the throng;
the men give up their employments, and lying
on the ground smoking their pipes, or sitting
on the timber, or leaning on their rifles, they
listen attentively to the Gospel.   The preacher
is short and forcible—he speaks to them of
"righteousness, temperance, and judgment to
come"—he tells them of a Saviour and a friend.
He uses their own language, and his illustrations are borrowed from the scenes and avoca-
tions with which they are most familiar.   I have
seen in such a group the bold eye suffused with
moisture, and the lips moving in a prayer
learned perhaps long ago at some pious mother's
knee.   And a horny hand would grasp that of
the minister, and lips unused to mild words

would thank him for his sermon; and if no deeper feelings were stirred, and the goodness were but as the passing cloud, the next six days would tell of pulpit influence. Deeds of unwonted kindness would be performed, the bowie-knife would remain unsheathed, the too frequent oath would be clumsily restrained, and society would be the better for that sermon though it had nothing of pulpit dignity, intellectual effort, or artistic arrangement about it. Whenever a few settlers congregate throughout the Far West, they have the Gospel preached to them statedly, or occasionally, and one secret of the remarkable effect of preaching in those regions is the adaptation of language and ideas. The people are not called upon to listen to a discussion on an unfamiliar subject in language which is unsuited to their comprehension. I have heard a preacher, while addressing a wild audience on the Upper Mississippi, borrow his illustrations from the traffic and customs of the river, and make use of this (to his hearers) most forcible expression: "Oh, my friends, Jesus Christ is the only tree to tie to;" a simile full of meaning to all who are acquainted with those waters. The boats moor to trees on the river bank, which sometimes are undermined by the action of the water and give way, while others bear the strain and occasionally have their capabilities denoted by a notched mark. Again, in a new settlement on the borders of one of the great prairies, I heard a Baptist minister conclude a most earnest and effective sermon, on " Enter ye in at the strait gate," with these words:—" You *will* make a circumbendibus; I want you to make a bee-line to heaven;" in allusion to the prevalent mode of traversing a pathless prairie or forest.

In the South the preaching is still the same, more polished perhaps in its language than in the West, but earnest and Evangelical. There, as elsewhere, the pulpit seeks to convince men of sin, and that the Gospel is blessed in the South I do not doubt any more than that its progress is hindered by one important omission. The Southern ministers denounce drunkenness and other vices; dishonest dealing, worldliness, the love of display, &c; but the sin of Slavery, and the sins which arise out of it, pass unrebuked. We hear of other sins as elsewhere; but the one terrible system which denies to 4,000,000 human beings the right of indissoluble marriage, and the sacredness of the parental tie, which sustains an iniquitous internal Slave-trade, which vitiates alike public and private morals, this the pulpit protects and fosters, and denounces as " sceptics" or " abolitionists" all who assert on the broad basis of moral right the equality of the human race. With this exception no aspersion can be cast on the Southern pulpit, for no country possesses a more compact mass of orthodox preaching. The Slaves in very many localities participate in the privileges of a pure Gospel preached in a manner which accords with their simplicity and ignorance, Evangelical in its sentiments, though often, to our ideas, painfully grotesque in its language.

The first great characteristic of American preaching is its serious earnestness. Men preach as if they felt the responsibility of the ministry and the value of souls. " We believe and therefore speak," appears to give the directness which their preaching certainly has. They preach as if the lost state of man and salvation through Christ were the grandest and most outstanding realities in the universe, and strive to prepare dying men for death, judgment, and eternity. A second characteristic is its faithfulness. The ministers are not intimidated, as some persons in England suppose, by the rich and influential in their congregations who dislike the truth. They faithfully preach Christ crucified; they urge upon their hearers to repent and denounce the sins of every class and profession and of professing Christians with a boldness and plainness which I have never heard equalled. A third, is its simplicity. The preachers generally take plain texts and prefer to give their natural and obvious meaning rather than anything far-fetched or philosophical. Familiar, vigorous, and perspicuous language is generally preferred to the ornate and rhetorical. Men preach to educated hearers in language which is perfectly intelligible to the uneducated. A fourth and very marked characteristic is that American preaching dwells much on immediate reconciliation with God. The becoming reconciled to God " to-day " is continually urged upon sinners. The call to repent and believe the Gospel immediately is for ever sounding in the ears of those who are recognized as " unconverted," and no delay is excused, and no excuse is accepted. Christ is preached, not Christianity; and the immediate acceptance of his atonement is constantly urged. A fifth characteristic is that it is systematic. That is, that the highest style of Evangelical preaching strives to maintain a proper connection between the discourses successively delivered from the same pulpit, and to make every statement and argument bear upon and strengthen that which precedes it, so as to tend to the final results of demonstration and clearness rather than to present separated and isolated statements of truth. A sixth characteristic is that it is eminently practical. The unconverted are urged to repentance and faith, and Christians are incessantly directed to " walk worthy of the vocation whereunto they are called," to live for the glory of God, and the salvation of men. Of late years this idea has had an ever-increasing prominence given to it in preaching, that every Christian in every sphere of life is under an obligation so to live, that by his influence, conversation, and example, he may promote the welfare of men. The line which separates the Church from the world is also drawn so distinctly, that none can doubt on which side of it they are to be found. A seventh characteristic is that it dwells much on the work of the Holy

Spirit. The idea of the importance of his work and office is a dominant one in American preaching, and the need of his work of conversion, the necessity of his co-operation with the setting forth of the Gospel, and the promise of the Spirit as the great and permanent ascension gift of Christ, are among the most prominent of pulpit themes, and have been so for a hundred years. In addition to these seven characteristics, it may be stated that American preaching is very doctrinal and very philosophical in the highest sense of the word, and consequently contains all the elements of power.

To these characteristics it may be added that full expositions of doctrine are given, the " Whole Counsel of God is declared," together with minute indications of Christian practice. Nothing is left to be taken for granted. Large congregations everywhere listen with the most earnest attention to sermons which are remarkable for nothing but the faithfulness with which the preacher tells his hearers of their sins, the energy with which he dissects the characters of the hypocrite and the self-deceiver, and holds up in the broad glare of Gospel day the flimsy, threadbare robe of man's fancied righteousness;

and the persuasive earnestness with which he
implores his hearers to be reconciled to God
through Jesus Christ, probing the inmost recesses of man's nature, and speaking not only
from the head to the intellect, but from the
depths of the heart itself to the sentient seat of
conscience and feeling in every hearer before
him. That literary efforts and intellectual exercise do occasionally occupy the pulpits I do not
mean to deny, or that by some of the Episcopalian clergy more importance is attached to out-
ward observances than the word of truth war-
rants; but taking the great mass of preaching
throughout America, I believe it is in a marked
degree free from doctrinal errors and unscrip-
tural perversions, and that it is of that character
which " through faith is able to make men wise
unto salvation." It is distinguished by a zeal
and a desire for the conversion of souls, accom-
panied with an extreme faithfulness in the denunciation of general, congregational, and individual sins, which combine to give it an efficiency, and to produce an energetic, active state
of Christianity, at which conventional religion
may shudder, and which formalistic churchman-

M

162   CHARACTERISTICS OF

ship may condemn, but to which we have nothing comparable.

But zealous and ardent as the American pulpit is, its zeal must not be praised at the expense of its power. There are names inferior to none which are already well known in England. There is Bishop McIlvaine, with his intellectual power and apostolic zeal; Finney, with his calm pleading and logical definition; Dr. Tyng, with his " tongue of fire ;" Cheever, with his forceful denunciations of wrong, which have eaten into men's souls like red-hot iron; Barnes, whose writings are esteemed a text-book of theology; Henry Ward Beecher, whose eccentric genius, burning words, and eloquent " Life Thoughts " have won him an almost European celebrity; and a goodly list of names behind. It is a revived ministry which makes a revived Church—it is the preaching of a living Gospel, and not of dogmatic theology and intellectual abstractions, which gives life to the souls of men; and much of the good which America possesses is to be traced to the undisguised Gospel which her pulpits proclaim, and to the zeal and consistency of her clergy. There are thousands of ministers in the United States

who aim neither to perform great literary prodigies, to fill their aisles and lobbies, to produce
a sentimental religious influence, but to convert
their hearers; who regard each undying soul in
their congregations with the love and yearning
of Him who came to seek and to save the lost;
—who have no earthly ambitions, and no cause
on earth to serve but that for which they are
ministers, and who serve it by a consistent life
and an ardent devotion, looking for no other
reward than the many-jewelled crown which
shall be placed on the heads of all who have
turned many to righteousness by our Lord
Himself in the great day of His appearing.

CHAPTER X.—*General Criticisms.*

N England there are two classes of thinkers on America—the Tories, who speculate gloomily upon the onward tendencies and unshackled progress of the Western Republic, and profess to see in its government nothing but universal corruption, in its religion unbridled latitudinarianism, and in its material progress only the portentous sign of its approaching overthrow; and the Ultra-Liberals, who see a political and religious Utopia on the other side of the Atlantic, in equal electoral districts, universal suffrage, and vote by ballot, an unfailing panacea for the woes of our smitten humanity, and in the voluntary system, the only true ecclesiastical polity. The sentiments of the first are in danger of leading to a zealous conservatism of English abuses, and those of the last to a shallow and reckless empiricism, which would practically subvert old systems before new ones had been thought out to fill the void; and neither have formed a true estimate of America. It is doubtless difficult for men who have been brought up under the shadow of a throne of which a splendid hierarchy is one of the chief supports to realize a national apart from a governmental religion, and that Churches amenable to no Privy Council Judicial Committees can be secure in doctrine and discipline. In a country whose traditions tend to preserve the social stratification of class separation, and where the voice of the masses has only been heard on a few memorable occasions, which are suggestive of "special constables," it is hard for men to realize that every adult man may be trusted with the franchise without endangering the whole political fabric and the peace of society. Neither is it surprising that the opposite party, sanguine in expectation, and smarting under the memories of former grievances, should overestimate the advantages of American institutions, and believe that a reorganization of Church and State upon their model would be the dawn of a bright day of progress. The

institutions of America are suited to America;
under none but a popular government could her
material progress have been so rapid; under no
system but the voluntary system could her religious advancement have kept pace with her
growth, and universal suffrage wedded to *high
class universal education* has been, and is, one of
her chief safeguards. I wish to make this final
survey of religion in America as impartial as
possible, avoiding either of the extremes before alluded to; and in the first place I will
remark upon the praiseworthy characteristics of
those Churches which are termed Orthodox.

Few things connected with religion in America make a stronger impression upon a stranger
than the comparative absence of sectarianism,
the harmonious action of the ministers, and the
social intercourse which exists irrespective of
denominational differences.   In the various
aggressive schemes the ministers cordially unite;
in most of the orthodox denominations they ex-
change pulpits; they meet in union prayer-
meetings, and in very many cities and towns it
is the regular practice for the ministers of all
denominations to hold a weekly meeting for
mutual encouragement and counsel, and for

arranging co-operative plans for the good of
their location.   This intercourse is everywhere
productive of very happy results.   The union
is public and practical also, and tends to place
minor differences in the background.   Many
of the denominations unite in schemes for the
conversion of men, such as the Bible Society,
the Sunday-school Union, the American Board
of Foreign Missions, and the Tract Society.
In social intercourse persons of the same intellectual and social affinities mingle without a
shade of difference.   The social standing of no
person is lowered on denominational grounds.
The Churches make a common cause against a
common foe, and the Holy Spirit has blessed
their united efforts.   It must, however, be re-
marked that one of the causes of sectarian feeling which exists in England does not exist in
the United States.   I do not believe that con-
scientious scruples and differences of opinion on
government or doctrine, though they must produce separation, will cause sectarianism.   The
evil rests on a lower ground—"of the earth,
earthy;"—those who have endowments are in
danger of being arrogant, and those who have
them not are in danger of being envious.   In

America there is no State Church; all denominations are on the same footing; the ministers of all are chosen by the members, who constitute the patrons, and none are under disabilities of any kind whatever. There is doubtless a good deal of emulation among the Churches, but it is usually productive of happy results, and the jealousies or heartburnings which occasionally arise are of short duration, and are scarcely observable in the warm feelings of fraternal, loving Christianity which pervade the Churches.

Another feature is the comparative strictness of Church membership. The form of "joining the Church" varies. Among some it is by confirmation, in others by baptism, in others by a solemn public profession, but in all the necessity of a change of heart is recognized, and the public profession is considered, in the eyes of the world, as a renunciation of its vanities and associations. In the Episcopal Church the rite of confirmation is not administered, as with us, as a matter of course, at the age of fifteen or sixteen. It is by common consent deferred until the person desiring to receive it is ready to " take up the cross and follow Christ." On each occasion when I witnessed the ceremony

fully half of the persons receiving the rite were
in middle life, and some had even reached old
age. In some cases, and universally among the
Presbyterians, when a person desires to join
the Church the pastor reports the matter to the
Church session, and the candidate has to appear
before that body, which consists of the pastor
and elders. In the Congregational and Baptist
Churches the candidate has to appear before
the body of the members of the Church and
state his reasons for the faith which he professes. In all cases the preparatory examination is very strict, and "joining the Church" is
considered an act of separation from the world.
When a man has once become a Church member, i. e. a communicant, he renders himself
liable to strict discipline; admonition or excom-
munication follow various kinds of inconsistency,
and it may fairly be presumed that the most of
the Church members are true Christians.

As a chapter was devoted to the subject of
preaching it is only necessary to remark that a
pious membership ensures evangelical preaching,
as the members are the patrons. The consistency of ministers is a very marked feature,
and it must be great indeed when the Argus-

eyed scrutiny of the press can find so little of an opposite nature. They are generally looked up to, and have a vast influence. They keep themselves wholly separate from the world, and, as a general rule, avoid all social questionable ground. No ministers are more deserving of respect, and the testimony of their conduct is equal to the testimony of their preaching. For a man to take upon him the ministerial office merely to obtain an honourable place in society, or gain a decent livelihood, would be universally reprobated; and if anything could be more generally contemned, it would be an inconsistent life on the part of anyone who had undertaken such solemn responsibilities. This consistent ministry is the greatest of all blessings to the Churches, and is one of the great instruments for securing the morals of the community and the stability of the government. One subject, which is somewhat of a distasteful one, must in justice be alluded to. The ministers are generally total abstainers, for the reason given in 1 Corinthians viii. 13. They placed themselves at the head of the total abstinence movement at a period when habits of intoxication were committing great ravages in the country, and have met with success which could not have been foretold. It is not respectable for a minister to indulge in stimulants, it is disrespectful to offer them to him, and to such an extent is this carried that even in the South, where the drinking customs resemble those of England, the presence of a totally abstaining minister frequently prevents wine from being placed on the table at social gatherings out of mere courteous respect. The prodigious decrease in intemperance, and the contempt which attaches in the New England States to the use of stimulants, are monuments of ministerial self-denial. When we view the intemperance of England, the height to which it has attained, the results of crime and degradation which attend it, and the effectual barrier which it opposes to the progress of religion among the poor, it is impossible to help recalling the great social reformation effected in America, and querying whether praying against it and preaching against it by our clergy will ever have the effect of a similar practical movement on their part. The attitude of the American Churches on this subject is worthy of consideration.

Another feature is the excellence of the Sab-

bath-school system. The American Sabbath-
schools at the present time are supposed to
contain three million pupils, and over three
hundred thousand teachers. They embrace a
great mass of the population of *all classes* up to
adult age, and form a gigantic and ever-expand-
ing organization, training everywhere a God-
fearing people, and in newly-settled districts
preparing the way for Churches and ministers.
The American Sunday-school Union, the board
of managers of which is composed of laymen of
the various Evangelical denominations, is one of
the most successful of the Evangelistic agencies
in America. This society, in 1830, resolved to
establish a Sabbath-school in every neighbourhood in the Western States that was without
one, and in 1833 it adopted a like resolution
with respect to the Southern States. It em-
ploys about 350 missionaries, of whom 250 are
students in theological seminaries, and their
work is to traverse the country through its vast
extent, revitalizing decaying schools, establish-
ing new ones, and encouraging all. The object
of the society is twofold; to provide the young
with oral instruction, and with suitable reading
at home. It has published 813 volumes of books

for libraries, exclusive of an infinite variety of educational works, magazines, and journals. Besides this association, the Episcopalians, Baptists, Methodists, and Lutherans, have Sunday-school Unions, and the State of Massachusetts has one of its own. The Sunday-school libraries, which are universally connected with Sunday-schools, are fostering a taste for the best class of reading among the rising youth and the adult population of the country. The scholars receive one or two volumes each every Sabbath, to be returned on the Sabbath following, and so great is the demand for the valuable publications of these societies, that their sales are nearly to the extent of half a million of dollars annually. Each school is under a superintendent, and the teachers for the most part are pious people. It is no uncommon thing to find persons filling the highest offices in the State, governors, members of Congress, judges, eminent lawyers, mayors of cities, who are Sunday-school teachers. The late President Harrison, on the very Sabbath before he left his home to become his country's chief magistrate, gave a last lesson to the class which he had instructed for several years. The Sabbath-school in America is a highly-valued and distinct organization, and derives an added importance from circumstances which must be briefly alluded to.

The American Common School system of education may safely be stated to be the noblest and most efficient in the world, and well worthy of an enlightened people in the world's most enlightened age. Although the Bible is generally used as a reading book in these schools, and although a pious and judicious teacher, if he confines himself to its fundamental truths, can give as much religious instruction as he pleases, the system must be regarded as one of *secular education*. It is not within my province to express an opinion as to the policy or justice of making no provision for religious instruction, but I would remind those who condemn the system pursued, that difficulties beset the subject of which they can hardly form a conception here; and that in schools supported by a rate levied indiscriminately on all to form a course of instruction which could bear the name of a religious one, meeting the views of all and clashing with the consciences and prejudices of none, is manifestly impossible. As it would be, therefore, neither possible nor right to educate

the children in any denominational creed, or to
instruct them in any particular doctrinal system,
the religious public has felt that there is no
tenable ground between thorough religious instruction and the broadest toleration, and has
been compelled by circumstances to make the
best of the latter course. In the full conviction
that the bestowment of an intellectual culture,
which draws forth and adds to the power of the
mind without giving it any helm to guide it, is
to increase the capacity without diminishing the
propensity to do evil, the Churches of the
United States have devoted their energies to
train the young in the fear of God by the most
extensive and the most efficient Sabbath-school
system in the world.

It has been brought as a charge against the
voluntary system in America, that those who
are unable or unwilling to pay for religious
ordinances will be left without them. This
charge is completely unfounded. I have no
hesitation in saying that under the voluntary
system in the United States the poor are more
systematically and universally sought out than
under the parochial system in our English cities.
The American Churches are singularly aggres-

sive. There are the Sunday-school Unions, which are continually organizing new schools; the Home Missionary Societies, which are ever carrying the means of grace into destitute districts and organizing Churches; the Southern Aid Society, which takes religious destitution in the South as its sole field; the Tract Society, with its gigantic system of colportage, and several minor agencies. The Churches are equally energetic in local efforts. In New York, Philadelphia, and the other cities, the rich support mission Churches and mission agencies among the poor to an extent that is perfectly surprising. It is no exaggeration to state that there is not a house in New York and Philadelphia which has not had the Gospel brought within its doors by an organized system of visitation from which even palatial mansions are not exempt. A mission Church among the poor is often a part of the organization of wealthy congregations. A single congregation in one city has erected five of these. Special agencies are actively at work. In Cincinnati and Philadelphia tents capable of holding 2,000 persons itinerate for the purpose of Sabbath-day services. In New York the three largest edifices

in the city, the Academy of Music, the National
Theatre, and the Cooper Institute, are opened
on Sunday evenings by some of the most gifted
ministers of the city, for the purpose of accom-
modating those who are too poor or too preju-
diced to go to church, and similar influences
are at work everywhere. There is no person
in any of the settled districts who cannot have,
if he desires it, the privilege of religious worship; and missionaries are busy in the streets
and lanes of the cities seeking to compel the
outcasts to come in.

Another feature of the active religion of
America is the energy with which foreign missions are prosecuted. There is a missionary
spirit among the congregations which is kept
alive by means as yet untried in England. Each
year the theological seminaries send forth numerous young men 'of high attainments to the
mission-fields, and missionary labour takes a
very high position both in the estimation of the
press and the public. The number of candidates presenting themselves for work among
the heathen, and the elevated position which
that work occupies in public estimation, are

N

among the surest indications of the influence of
vital Christianity.

After these eulogistic remarks, to which many
more might be added, I will point out a few of
the defects which are to be recognized in the
American Churches, not in a spirit of detrac-
tion, but in that of candid criticism. I am
inclined to place dalliance with Slavery first,
although quite aware of the political difficulties
which attend interference with the system, and
of the threat of disunion which the South hangs,
like the sword of Damocles, over the heads of
all who condemn Slavery. The pro-slavery
attitude of many of the congregations in New
York, Pennsylvania, Ohio, and Indiana, is much
to be condemned. The Northern ministers are
living in States in which the question has been
set at rest for ever; they have never been ex-
posed to the baneful and insidious influences of
Slavery; and if they do not regard it as their
duty to utter a protest against it, it is at least
to be expected that they would remain neutral.
On the contrary, many of them speak directly
or indirectly in its favour; they publish books
containing " Southside Views " of Slavery, they
hold fellowship with it, and while deprecating

any " political allusions" from the pulpit to it on one side, they practise them on the other. Among the 800 ministers of New York and Philadelphia, few are found bold enough to denounce the connection which many of their congregations have with the slave system, or to interpret practically our Saviour's golden rule. Albert Barnes, the learned commentator, and Beecher and Cheever of New York, boldly testify against Slavery; but the faithfulness of the latter in condemning the sins of the Churches in connection with it has kept his congregation in a continual ferment, and his resignation has been more than once demanded; for no offence is less likely to meet with lenient treatment than a testimony against Slavery.

That large and catholic association the American Tract Society, admirable as is the most of its work, is also guilty in this respect. In republishing foreign books they are subjected to a systematic revision and mutilation, whereby all passages bearing unfavourably upon Slavery are excised. If Mary Lundie Duncan, or Dr. Harris, or Mrs. Isabella Graham, are found to have classed Slavery with the evils of the age, the word is erased; or if a writer rejoices over

West India emancipation, and expresses a hope that Slavery will soon be classed among the obsolete tyrannies of the earth, the sentence is skilfully deprived of the obnoxious passage. Recently, under the pressure of exhortation from without, the Tract Society resolved to publish a series of tracts treating of the evils and the duties arising out of Slavery, but the resolution was never carried into effect. So sensitive are Southern Christians upon this subject that this course would have led to their severance from the society, and the South would no longer have been a field for its operations. After a protracted meeting and a stormy discussion the committee returned to its former policy. It is impossible not to condemn its timorous conduct in the first instance, and the *principle* of non-interference with a recognized evil; but hampered as the society is by prior resolves, its *practice* may admit of some extenuating considerations.

Secondly, it is to be observed that the world enters into the American Churches in the shape of the desire for wealth and a love of display. This is evidenced in the number of the edifices for worship which are frequently built at an extravagant cost, and abound in stained glass, rich carving, paintings or transparencies, and marble altars, everything, in short, to attract and distract the eye. In many of the churches the singing is exquisite artistically, but not as a part of worship, and professional singers are engaged at a great expense, who would resent any congregational interference with their performance. The love of splendid residences, fine equipages and furniture, and of costly and fashionable apparel, is also found within the Churches, more particularly among the Episcopalians, to an extent which appears inconsistent with the separation from the world and from the " lust of the flesh, the lust of the eyes, and the pride of life," from which our Saviour exhorts us to flee. I am inclined to believe that there are many persons making a Christian profession who desire the reputation of *millionaires* rather than of disciples. Again, the love of display is evidenced by the desire in some of the congregations to vie with each other in the eloquence of their ministers, and rhetoric will occasionally command a higher salary than more useful qualifications. Men take a pride in great sermons, and feel a self-complacency in their

selection of a minister when they have wrung
a eulogy on his ability from some strange hearer.
There is no *social* equality, as some suppose, in
the Great Republic. Society is there regulated
by social and intellectual affinities—the most
rational rule I am inclined to believe. Yet, as
a further criticism, I must say that I have observed in some places, especially in one of the
most populous cities, a want of that friendliness
among members of the same Christian Church
which is desirable, and a pride of birth, station,
and wealth, which is scarcely consistent.

Again, while the standards of doctrines in the
orthodox Churches are strictly scriptural, in one
section of the religious world there is a species
of false charity to doctrinal error which is calculated to have an injurious effect upon the
young. The prototype of this leniency towards
error is to be seen in Henry Ward Beecher,
who, in his glittering "Life Thoughts" and eloquent addresses, has identified himself with the
poet who writes—

> "For forms of faith let senseless zealots fight,
> He can't be wrong whose life is in the right."

Again, I think that a great many Christian

people are too much inclined to delegate to
others the religious training of their children.
Sabbath-schools and Bible-classes are admirable
things, but they are calculated to supplement,
rather than supersede, that home-training, those
family Bible-readings, those Bible-stories told
in simple language, those simple prayers by
Christian mothers over infant faults and infant
sorrows which do more than anything else to
train up virtuous men and virtuous women, and
sustain that paternal authority which is the
basis of true government. The love of excitement and the restlessness which certainly do
characterize the American character, are fostered
rather than discouraged in youth, and much of
the flippancy and ultra-independence among
children and young people which many strangers
have observed appears to me to be referable to
the want of complete home discipline and religious training. There are other things which
are defective in the Churches, but they are peculiar to human nature rather than to America.
There is an idea in England that the religious
systems of America are on the high-pressure
principle, and that excitement is one of their
prominent features; but I am not disposed to

assent to this if it is meant as a condemnation. I think that what many religious people stigmatize as "high-pressure" and "excitement" is significant only of vitality, earnest Evangelistic effort, and progressive development; of a state of things faulty indeed in many respects, but which many in England are now desiring. The bonds between England and America cannot be drawn too close, and as fresh information on the state of religion in America is diffused among us our sympathies will be quickened and our energies aroused, and those on both sides of the Atlantic who hold "one Lord, one Faith, and one Baptism," will be united further in Evangelistic effort.

CONCLUSION.

I COMMENCED this little volume resolving "nought to extenuate or set down aught in malice," and yet it will doubtless meet with criticism from two opposite quarters. Some English readers, presuming on their knowledge derived from occasional notices in the English papers of discreditable incidents in America, will think that I have painted it *couleur de rose,* while others in America will accuse me of having written on many subjects with prejudice, and on that of Slavery with actual malice. My English critics must understand that I have written solely upon the Churches and their influence, and that it is not my intention to depict society generally. Yet I would suggest that it is as unfair to judge of society, and of the code of morals by which it is governed, by the Sickles' tragedy, or by a murderous duel or Lynch-law execution in the wilds of Arkansas or Texas, as it would be for a stranger to judge of the manners of the English from our assize or police reports. Property is universally secure in the United States, and so are the lives of all peaceable citizens. This result, which is the end of all legislation, is produced in a sparsely settled territory, about the size of Europe, principally by the influence of religion. To my Transatlantic friends I reply, that I owe them no apology for anything that I have said, and I esteem them more highly than to believe that they would prefer servile adulation and indiscriminate eulogy to honest criticism. Many and sacred are the ties which bind me to America, and I cordially unite with all who love her in thankfulness for the good things with which she has been blessed. With respect to minor defects, all who are really acquainted with the Churches will agree with me, and I have pointed them out in pursuance of an intention to write the whole truth. In regard to Slavery, which I have condemned in terms which will be themselves condemned, all true-hearted Americans must join me at least in regretting that such an element of weakness should underlie the national strength, and in an earnest longing (on political and social if not on higher grounds) that ere long American Slavery may be classed with the obsolete tyrannies of the earth, and that the starry banner of the Republic may wave over none but the free.

The present condition of America is annually attracting greater attention in this country, and more kindly feelings are arising between England and the Republic out of which practical good must ensue. The fires of an old jealousy are dying out before a larger faith and a more comprehensive charity. England is forgetting Ticonderoga and Saratoga, the multiplied defeats and final surrender of her armies; and

America hears the roll of the British drum without a wish to tarnish the glory of an empire on which the sun never sets. Each nation has the same mission—to bless the world with Christianity and peace, with liberty and enlightenment. May God grant that a less holy rivalry may never exist between them! The prosperity of England is dear to America; our reverses thrill the heart of the whole nation with sympathy, and our triumphs create a throb of pride from the shores of the Atlantic to the Rocky Mountains. The waste howling Atlantic itself is bridged by mutual sympathies and prayers, and a common Christianity and a common mission are cementing the union yet more closely than common commercial interests.

To America are now gravitating, as never before to another centre, all nations, tongues, and tendencies. Planted in the strength and light of truth, her Churches have needed no reformation or purification by martyr blood. Aided by the favourable circumstances in which they were placed, they have grasped the grand truths of Christianity with a more definite aim and a larger promise of success than those of any other portion of the Christian world. To

them, cut off from the embarrassments while
reaping the heritage of the past, a mighty and
responsible mission has been given. The reform
of society by the Christian faith, the transform-
ation of society into the kingdom of Christ is
their great work, and in this are to be found the
aim and sum of the whole history of our race.
The point has never before been raised as it is
now in America. If the preceding sketch of
the Churches and their influences be at all
correct, it will be seen that the faith to which
the land was dedicated in its historic prime is
now advancing with its growth throughout all
its borders in spite of political corruption, pantheistic allurements, infidel propagandism, and
all the other obstacles which the Power of Evil
places in the way of that Gospel which is destined to overthrow both him and them. America
is rapidly assuming a prominence among empires to fulfil God's purposes towards the human
race; and while in the fickle fortunes of men
we read the sure order of an unchanging plan,
in the growth of states, under such conditions as
have been mentioned, we may as surely trace
the unhasting yet unresting progress of a kingdom ordained ere time began, to be completed

when time shall be no more, and the approach
of a day when earth's monarchies shall be over-
thrown, and earth's republics shall bow before
the sway of a despotic sceptre, and the crown
of universal empire shall be placed upon the
head of our Lord Jesus Christ, of whom it is
recorded in the sure word of a prophecy which
never yet has failed, that every tongue shall
confess that He is Lord to the glory of God the
Father.

THE END.

CHISWICK PRESS :—PRINTED BY C. WHITTINGHAM,
TOOKS COURT, CHANCERY LANE.

Religion in America
Series II

An Arno Press Collection

Adler, Felix. **Creed and Deed: A** Series of Discourses. New York, 1877.

Alexander, Archibald. **Evidences of the Authenticity, Inspiration, and Canonical Authority of the Holy Scriptures.** Philadelphia, 1836.

Allen, Joseph Henry. **Our Liberal Movement in Theology:** Chiefly as Shown in Recollections of the History of Unitarianism in New England. 3rd edition. Boston, 1892.

American Temperance Society. **Permanent Temperance Documents of the American Temperance Society.** Boston, 1835.

American Tract Society. **The American Tract Society Documents,** 1824-1925. New York, 1972.

Bacon, Leonard. **The Genesis of the New England Churches.** New York, 1874.

Bartlett, S[amuel] C. **Historical Sketches of the Missions of the American Board.** New York, 1972.

Beecher, Lyman. **Lyman Beecher and the Reform of Society:** Four Sermons, 1804-1828. New York, 1972.

[Bishop, Isabella Lucy Bird.] **The Aspects of Religion in the United States of America.** London, 1859.

Bowden, James. **The History of the Society of Friends in America.** London, 1850, 1854. Two volumes in one.

Briggs, Charles Augustus. **Inaugural Address and Defense,** 1891-1893. New York, 1972.

Colwell, Stephen. **The Position of Christianity in the United States,** in Its Relations with Our Political Institutions, and Specially with Reference to Religious Instruction in the Public Schools. Philadelphia, 1854.

Dalcho, Frederick. **An Historical Account of the Protestant Episcopal Church, in South-Carolina,** from the First Settlement of the Province, to the War of the Revolution. Charleston, 1820.

Elliott, Walter. **The Life of Father Hecker.** New York, 1891.

Gibbons, James Cardinal. **A Retrospect of Fifty Years.** Baltimore, 1916. Two volumes in one.

Hammond, L[ily] H[ardy]. **Race and the South:** Two Studies, 1914-1922. New York, 1972.

Hayden, A[mos] S. **Early History of the Disciples in the Western Reserve, Ohio;** With Biographical Sketches of the Principal Agents in their Religious Movement. Cincinnati, 1875.

Hinke, William J., editor. **Life and Letters of the Rev. John Philip Boehm:** Founder of the Reformed Church in Pennsylvania, 1683-1749. Philadelphia, 1916.

Hopkins, Samuel. **A Treatise on the Millennium.** Boston, 1793.

Kallen, Horace M. **Judaism at Bay:** Essays Toward the Adjustment of Judaism to Modernity. New York, 1932.

Kreider, Harry Julius. **Lutheranism in Colonial New York.** New York, 1942.

Loughborough, J. N. **The Great Second Advent Movement:** Its Rise and Progress. Washington, 1905.

M'Clure, David and Elijah Parish. **Memoirs of the Rev. Eleazar Wheelock, D.D.** Newburyport, 1811.

McKinney, Richard I. **Religion in Higher Education Among Negroes.** New Haven, 1945.

Mayhew, Jonathan. **Observations on the Charter and Conduct of the Society for the Propagation of the Gospel in Foreign Parts;** Designed to Shew Their Non-conformity to Each Other. Boston, 1763.

Mott, John R. **The Evangelization of the World in this Generation.** New York, 1900.

Payne, Bishop Daniel A. **Sermons and Addresses,** 1853-1891. New York, 1972.

Phillips, C[harles] H. **The History of the Colored Methodist Episcopal Church in America:** Comprising Its Organization, Subsequent Development, and Present Status. Jackson, Tenn., 1898.

Reverend Elhanan Winchester: Biography and Letters. New York, 1972.

Riggs, Stephen R. **Tah-Koo Wah-Kan; Or, the Gospel Among the Dakotas.** Boston, 1869.

Rogers, Elder John. **The Biography of Eld. Barton Warren Stone, Written by Himself:** With Additions and Reflections. Cincinnati, 1847.

Booth-Tucker, Frederick. **The Salvation Army in America:** Selected Reports, 1899-1903. New York, 1972.

Satolli, Francis Archbishop. **Loyalty to Church and State.** Baltimore, 1895.

Schaff, Philip. **Church and State in the United States** or the American Idea of Religious Liberty and its Practical Effects with Official Documents. New York and London, 1888. (Reprinted from *Papers of the American Historical Association,* Vol. II, No. 4.)

Smith, Horace Wemyss. **Life and Correspondence of the Rev. William Smith, D.D.** Philadelphia, 1879, 1880. Two volumes in one.

Spalding, M[artin] J. **Sketches of the Early Catholic Missions of Kentucky;** From Their Commencement in 1787 to the Jubilee of 1826-7. Louisville, 1844.

Steiner, Bernard C., editor. **Rev. Thomas Bray:** His Life and Selected Works Relating to Maryland. Baltimore, 1901. (Reprinted from *Maryland Historical Society Fund Publication,* No. 37.)

To Win the West: Missionary Viewpoints, 1814-1815. New York, 1972.

Wayland, Francis and H. L. Wayland. **A Memoir of the Life and Labors of Francis Wayland, D.D., LL.D.** New York, 1867. Two volumes in one.

Willard, Frances E. **Woman and Temperance:** Or, the Work and Workers of the Woman's Christian Temperance Union. Hartford, 1883.